TWELFTH NIGHT

OR WHAT YOU WILL

By WILLIAM SHAKESPEARE

Preface and Annotations by
HENRY N. HUDSON

Introduction by
CHARLES HAROLD HERFORD

Twelfth Night, or What You Will
By William Shakespeare
Preface and Annotations by Henry N. Hudson
Introduction by Charles Harold Herford

Print ISBN 13: 978-1-4209-5342-8
eBook ISBN 13: 978-1-4209-5343-5

Cover Image: A detail of 'O, Mistress mine where are you roaming?', from 'Twelfth Night' by William Shakespeare (colour litho), Abbey, Edwin Austin (1852-1911) / Private Collection / Bridgeman Images.

Please visit *www.digireads.com*

CONTENTS

PREFACE.. 5

INTRODUCTION 7

TWELFTH NIGHT, OR WHAT YOU WILL

DRAMATIS PERSONAE 12

ACT I.

SCENE I. 13
SCENE II. 14
SCENE III. 16
SCENE IV. 21
SCENE V. 22

ACT II.

SCENE I. 31
SCENE II. 32
SCENE III. 33
SCENE IV. 39
SCENE V. 43

ACT III.

SCENE I. 50
SCENE II. 55
SCENE III. 58
SCENE IV. 59
SCENE V. 67

ACT IV.

SCENE I. 70
SCENE II. 73
SCENE III. 77

ACT V.

SCENE I. 79

Preface

Never printed, so far as is known, till in the folio of 1623. No contemporary notice of the play was discovered till the year 1828, when Collier, delving among the old papers in the Museum, lighted upon a manuscript *Diary*, written by one John Manningham, a barrister-at-law, who was entered at the Middle Temple in 1597. It seems that the benchers and members of the several law-schools in London, which were then called "Inns-of-Court," were wont to have annual feasts, and to enrich their convivialities with a course of wit and poetry. So, under date of February 2d, 1602, Manningham notes: "At our feast we had a play called *Twelfth Night, or What You Will*, much like *The Comedy of Errors*, or *Menechmi* in Plautus, but most like and near to that in the Italian called *Inganni*." The writer then goes on to state such particulars of the action as fully identify the play he saw with the one now in hand. Which ascertains that Shakespeare's *Twelfth Night* was performed before the members of the Middle Temple on the old Church festival of the Purification, formerly called Candlemas; an important link in the course of festivities that used to continue from Christmas to Shrovetide. The play was most likely fresh from the Poets hand when the lawyers thus had the pleasure of it; at least, the internal marks of allusion and style accord well with that supposal. In iii. 2, it is said of Malvolio, "He does smile his face into more lines than are in the new map, with the augmentation of the Indies." This is justly explained as referring to a famous multilineal map of the world, which appeared in 1598; the first map of the world in which the *Eastern Islands* were included. Again, in iii. 1, we have, "But, indeed, words are very rascals since bonds disgraced them"; alluding, apparently, to an order issued by the Privy Council in June, 1600, laying very tight restrictions upon the stage, and providing very severe penalties for any breach thereof.

The story upon which the more serious parts of *Twelfth Night* were founded appears to have been a general favourite before and during Shakespeare's time. It is met with in various forms and under various names in the Italian, French, and English literature of that period. The earliest form of it known to us is in Bandello's collection of novels. From the Italian of Bandello it was transferred, with certain changes and abridgments, into the French of Belleforest, and makes one in his collection of *Tragical Histories*. From one or the other of these sources the tale was borrowed again by Barnabe Rich, and set forth as *The History of Alpolonius and Silla*; making the second in his collection of tales entitled *Farewell to the Military Profession*, which was first printed in 1581.

Until the discovery of Manningham's *Diary*, Shakespeare was not supposed to have gone beyond these sources, and it was thought something uncertain to which of these he was most indebted for the raw material of his play. It is now held doubtful whether he drew from either of them. The passage I have quoted from that *Diary* notes a close resemblance of *Twelfth Night* to an Italian play "called *Inganni*." This has had the effect of directing attention to the Italian theatre in quest of his originals. Two comedies bearing the title of *Gl' Inganni* have been found, both of them framed upon the novel of Bandello, and both in print before the date of *Twelfth Night*. These, as also the three forms of the tale mentioned above, all agree in having a brother and sister, the latter in male attire, and the two bearing so close a resemblance in person and dress as to be indistinguishable; upon which circumstance some of the leading incidents are made to turn. In one of the Italian plays, the sister is represented as assuming the name of *Cesare*; which is so like *Cesario*, the name adopted by Viola in her disguise, that the one may well be thought to have suggested the other. Beyond this point, *Twelfth Night* shows no clear connection with either of those plays.

But there is a third Italian comedy, also lately brought to light, entitled *Gl' Inganntati*, which is said to have been first printed in 1537. Here the traces of indebtedness are much clearer and more numerous. I must content myself with abridging the Rev. Joseph Hunter's statement of the matter. In the Italian play, a brother and sister, named Fabritio and Lelia, are separated at the sacking of Rome in 1527. Lelia is carried to Modena, where a gentleman resides, named Flamineo, to whom she was formerly attached. She disguises herself as a boy, and enters his service. Flamineo, having forgotten his Lelia, is making suit to Isabella, a lady of Modena. The disguised Lelia is employed by him in his love-suit to Isabella, who remains utterly deaf to his passion, but falls desperately in love with the messenger. After a while, the brother Fabritio arrives at Modena, and his close resemblance to Lelia in her male attire gives rise to some ludicrous mistakes. At one time a servant of Isabella meets him in the street, and takes him to her house, supposing him to be the messenger; just as Sebastian is taken for Viola, and led to the house of Olivia. In due time the needful recognitions take place, whereupon Isabella easily transfers her affection to Fabritio, and Flamineo's heart no less easily ties up with the loving and faithful Lelia. In her disguise Lelia takes the name of Fabio; hence, most likely, the name of Fabian, who figures as one of Olivia's servants. The Italian play has also a character called Pasquella, to whom Maria corresponds; and another named *Malevolti*, of which *Malvolio* is a happy adaptation. All which fully establishes the connection between the Italian play and the English. As no translation of the former has been heard of, here again we have some reason for believing that the Poet could read Italian. As for the more comic portions of *Twelfth Night*,—those in which Sir Toby, Sir Andrew, and the Clown figure so delectably,—we have no reason to suppose that any part of them was borrowed.

HENRY HUDSON

1881.

Introduction

Twelfth Night was first printed in the Folio of 1623. Its history begins, for us, with the feast in the hall of the Middle Temple, 2nd February 1602, when it was apparently first performed. John Manningham, an otherwise undistinguished law-student, described the performance in terms which leave no doubt of its identity:—'At our feast wee had a play called Twelue night or what you will, much like the commedy of errores or Menechmi in Plautus, but most like and neere to that in Italian called Inganni, a good practise in it to make the steward beleeue his Lady widdowe was in love with him by counterfayting a letter, as from his Lady, in generall termes, telling him what shee liked best in him, and prescribing his gesture in smiling, his apparaile, etc. And then, when he came to practise, making him beleeue they tooke him to be mad.' The play thus described must have been comparatively new; it is incredible that the creation of Malvolio, in after years extraordinarily popular, should have already been familiar to the London stage when Manningham jotted down this essentially 'first-night' *précis* of his role. But there is no scrap of definite external evidence on the point; even Meres's omission (1598) of the play, in his well-known list of twelve Shakespearean pieces, does not quite decide that it had not yet been written, since his purpose was to exemplify, not to enumerate. Some recent critics have set the serious element in the play—the Viola story—at a much earlier date (c. 1593), chiefly on the grounds of its obvious relation to the stories of *The Two Gentlemen* and *The Comedy of Errors*, which it combines. Professor Conrad also dwells upon certain parallels in phrase to these and the other early comedies. Some of them are striking, but they are few, and largely balanced by other parallels to plays undoubtedly later; while the very similarity of the situations in which they occur would account for more resemblances of phrase than in fact exist. And the similarity of the stories only accentuates the differences in art. Only the most mechanical criticism can associate Viola chronologically with Julia in *The Two Gentlemen*, because they both serve their lovers in disguise. That the Malvolio story belongs to 1600-1 is, in any case, beyond question; some slight indications point to the latter year, especially the catch (sung in ii. 3.): 'Farewell, dear heart, since I must needs be gone," which first appeared in the *Book of Ayres*, 1601.

Of the later history of the play there is little to be said. The evidences of its popularity are more striking than abundant, and they concern only the comic plot. Ben Jonson paid the duel scene the compliment of an elaborate imitation in the similar scene between Sir Amorous La-Foole and Sir John Daw in *The Silent Woman* (1609). Marston's *What You Will* (pr. 1607) may possibly owe its title to Shakespeare,—it certainly owes nothing else,—and have led to the final disuse of this second title of his play in favour of the apparently meaningless first.[1] On the eve of the closing of the theatres, *Twelfth Night* was still, with *Henry IV.* and *Much Ado*, among the Shakespearean comedies which the town thronged to see:—

Ioe in a trice
The Cockpit Galleries, Boxes, all are full
To hear *Malvoglio*, that cross-garter'd gull.[2]

After the Restoration it was twice revived, in 1663 and 1669, and found great favour, though severely condemned by Pepys as 'but a silly play, and not at all related to the name or day.'

Manningham, as we have seen, thought the play 'much like the commedy of errores or Menechmi in Plautus, but most like and neere to that in Italian called Inganni.' *Inganni* was the title of several Italian plays, none of which has any further resemblance to *Twelfth Night* than the elementary one, that the heroine assumes male disguise. A play called *Gli Ingannati*, however, had also long existed, which contains the Viola story in its bare outlines. This was itself founded on a novel of Bandello's (ii. 36), which became still more widely known in the French paraphrase of Belleforest's *Histoires Tragiques*. An Elizabethan ex-soldier and pamphleteer, Barnaby Rich, told a story of similar type in 'Apollonius and Silla,' one of the eight 'Histories' of his *Farewell to the Militarie Profession* (1581). Both of these have in common an indistinguishable pair of twins, brother and sister, an irresponsive lover whom the sister pursues in male disguise, only to be employed by him in wooing a new mistress, who is finally consoled by the brother. Most of this matter reappears in the present comedy; but none of Shakespeare's comedies which can be said to borrow its plot at all owes less to the plot it borrows than does *Twelfth Night* to these gross, characterless, and in part ill-told tales.[3]

Above all, the character and situation of Viola are handled with an exquisite refinement of which none of them shows a trace. By making her fall in love with the stranger she has taken service with, instead of

---

[1] Fleay, *Ckron. Hist. of Shakespeare*, p. 219.

[2] Digges, verses prefixed to Shakespeare's *Poems*, 1640.

[3] Thus the essential fact of the likeness of brother and sister is mentioned by Rich, incidentally, after ten pages of narrative.

taking service with him in order to gratify her love, he avoids the situation—dear to romance, but supremely difficult in psychological drama—of a pure and high-bred woman pursuing her lover. The immense psychological and dramatic resource expended on this situation in *All's Well* shows how keenly Shakespeare then realised the problem imposed by the *motif* he had handled with so much facile grace in *The Two Gentlemen*. Helena and Viola may be said to divide between them the two roles—of self-assertion and self-effacement—daringly combined in the forsaken Julia. Helena pursues Bertram, but far from wooing another in his name, she uses his alien love-bonds to seal her own; Viola takes no single step to further her own hidden passion, but throws all her intelligence into the prosecution of her master's suit. In her we see for the first time the full beauty and pathos of faithful self-abnegation; her reticence is eloquent, and her eloquence, though it finds vent in two of the most thrilling descriptions of love in Shakespeare ('Make me a willow-cabin at your gate,' etc., and 'She never told her love'), ostensibly expresses the love of others, not her own. Outwardly, her relations with Olivia are like those of Rosalind with Phœbe, but the humour is here far more delicate and subdued; and Viola, far from exploiting the absurdities of Olivia's mistake in Rosalind's madcap vein, loyally conceals them, as by the adroit fiction, 'She took the ring of me' (ii. 2. 13), which deceived Malvolio and puzzled Malone.

Even the duke is treated without any disposition to accentuate the ludicrous aspect of his character and fortunes. He is among the figures which suggest that Shakespeare was attracted by the methods of Jonson. Luxurious emotions are the elements in which he lives; they run to seed in him like a 'Humour.' His opening words, 'If music be the food of love, play on,' incisively denote him. His love is not a master who subdues all his faculties and energies to its service, but an exquisite companion whom he dotes on and dallies with. He has no doubt a choice and graceful mind, and this saves him from ridicule, though hardly from contempt; but it serves rather to extract and formulate the finest essence of each passing moment than to draw obvious practical conclusions from facts. Hence the clown—no inapt observer—admirably prescribes for him a doublet of changeable taffeta, 'for thy mind is a very opal'; his speech flushes with the warmth and brilliance of each passing mood. He is sick of self-love, and his persistent courtship of Olivia rests upon a fatuous faith in his own prevailing fascination; but his egoism is amiable and effusive, and he enters easily into tender relations with his subordinates. Apolonius, in Rich's tale, has no kindness for his serving-man; but the charm of Cesario has conquered the sensitive duke long before the climax, and the discovery of his sex transforms it without effort into love. This change might seem to involve a modification of the climax of Rich's story, where Apolonius vows his man's death to avenge his lady's honour (Hazlitt's *Shakespearean Library*, i. 408). In Shakespeare's hands, however, the incident adds a piquant trait to the duke's character. His tenderness for the lad he dooms converts the act into a sacrifice, and invests it with a tragic significance full of relish to his artistic sense:—

> I'll sacrifice the lamb that I do love
> To spite a raven's heart within a dove.
> Why should I not, had I the heart to do it,
> Like to the Egyptian thief at point of death,
> Kill what I love?

Naturally, the momentary impulse to act dissolves in the cloud of emotions and fancies it evoked.

In the framework of this serious and poetic tale Shakespeare has introduced his most uproarious fun. But the comic plot of his invention is linked by pretty obvious affinities with the grave plot which he borrowed. The duke's fatuous courtship has grotesque counterparts in the suits of Malvolio and Sir Andrew; and Olivia is feigned to play the same part towards Malvolio which she played in tragic earnestness towards Viola. Olivia, though not the heroine of the drama, is the centre about which its several actions move, as her house is the scene of the richest complexities and contretemps of the comic plot. In variety of comic type, in richness of comic invention, *Twelfth Night* surpasses both the other two great comedies of Shakespeare's maturity; and here again we may suspect the influence of Jonson's great galleries of Humours. Never before, save in the almost contemporary Slender, had he exploited the humour of mental fatuity—a form of comedy less obvious, perhaps, to his large kindliness than to Jonson's intellectual hauteur. Sir Andrew and Slender are varieties of the 'country gull'— near kinsmen of Jonson's Master Stephen.[4] He is the bloodless, as Sir Toby is the full-blooded, type of disreputable, gluttonous, and bibulous knight,—comparatively realistic studies from the materials wrought into the great imaginative creation of Falstaff. 'Eating and drinking,' of which Sir Andrew rather thinks life consists, compose it as largely for Sir Toby as for Falstaff; but Sir Toby, with much of Falstaff's

---

[4] Among little traits in common between Sir Andrew and Stephen is pride in a well-hosed leg. Stephen thinks his leg 'would show in a silk hose' (*Every Man in His Humour*, i. 2), Andrew thinks his 'does indifferent well in a flame-coloured stock' (i. 3. 144). 'I had rather than forty shillings,' measures Andrew's desire for 'such a leg,' and Slender's for his forgotten book of songs. One of Sir Andrew's most effective touches of simplicity ('That's me, I warrant you. I knew 'twas I, for many do call me fool') is anticipated by Costard in *Love's Labour's Lost* (i. 1. 250, 251 f.). But Costard is as sly as he is simple, and gives as good as he gets in his intercourse with the courtly wits.

temperament, has little of his wit. The eternal conflict between civic morality and genial Bohemianism, which forms the ethical background of *Henry IV.*, is here more distinctly emphasised. So much so, that the character of Malvolio has notoriously been regarded as a symbol for the party whose regard for 'virtue' habitually found vent in a disparagement of 'cakes and ale.' 'Sometimes,' declares Maria, 'he is a kind of a Puritan.' She proceeds immediately to deny that he is a Puritan at all, or anything else but a time-server. Malvolio is drawn with too subtle a hand to be instructively defined by the 'Puritan' or any other label; and critics still discuss, and actors lament, the ambiguous complexion of his character and fate. It is not his Puritanism but his foppery that beguiles him into Maria's well-laid trap. And there are hints enough that we are not intended to take even his Puritan qualities altogether at Maria's or Sir Toby's valuation. Olivia values her 'poor fool,' and, after all explanations, resents his discomfiture; while he himself grows in dignity as his persecution grows in violence. The Malvolio of the madhouse is a figure some degrees less comic than the Malvolio of the gardenscene, and his indignant yet tempered protest, when released, insensibly excites in the modern reader a sympathy which removes him for the moment from the region of comedy altogether. In a household so richly furnished with comic types as Olivia's, the professed humorist plays a minor part. Feste, the clown, is distinguished among Shakespeare's fools by his comparative realism; he is not sublimated and poetised like Touchstone, but renders, literally enough, the regulation buffooneries of the typical court jester. In one point he stands alone, as the singer of the songs scattered through the play, which so finely touch its various moods—languishing sentiment, rollicking gaiety, and mischief. It contributes something to its harmonious unity that the mocking reminiscence of the 'old Vice with his dagger of lath' springs from the same excellent breast which had recalled for the solace of the sentimental duke antique memories of another order—the old plain song:

> That dallies with the innocence of love
> Like the old age.

CHARLES HAROLD HERFORD

1901.

TWELFTH NIGHT, OR WHAT YOU WILL

Dramatis Personae

ORSINO, *Duke of Illyria.*
SEBASTIAN, *a young Gentleman, brother to Viola.*
ANTONIO, *a Sea Captain, friend to Sebastian.*
A SEA CAPTAIN, *friend to Viola.*
VALENTINE, *Gentleman attending on the Duke.*
CURIO, Gentleman attending on the Duke.
SIR TOBY BELCH, *Uncle of Olivia.*
SIR ANDREW AGUECHEEK

MALVOLIO, *Steward to Olivia.*
FABIAN, *Servant to Olivia.*
CLOWN, *Servant to Olivia.*

OLIVIA, *a rich Countess.*
VIOLA, *in love with the Duke.*
MARIA, *Olivia's Woman.*

Lords, Priests, Sailors, Officers, Musicians, and other Attendants.

SCENE: *A City in Illyria; and the Sea-coast near it.*

ACT I.

SCENE I.

An Apartment in the DUKE'*s Palace.*

[*Enter* DUKE, CURIO, LORDS; MUSICIANS *attending.*]

DUKE. If music be the food of love, play on,
    Give me excess of it; that, surfeiting,
    The appetite may sicken and so die.
    That strain again! it had a dying fall;[1]
    O, it came o'er my ear like the sweet south,
    That breathes upon a bank of violets,
    Stealing and giving odour.—Enough; no more;
    'Tis not so sweet now as it was before.
    O spirit of love, how quick and fresh art thou!
    That, notwithstanding thy capacity
    Receiveth as the sea, nought enters there,
    Of what validity[2] and pitch soever,
    But falls into abatement and low price
    Even in a minute! so full of shapes is fancy,[3]
    That it alone is high-fantastical.
CURIO. Will you go hunt, my lord?
DUKE. What, Curio?
CURIO. The hart.
DUKE. Why, so I do, the noblest that I have:
    O, when mine eyes did see Olivia first,
    Methought she purg'd the air of pestilence;
    That instant was I turn'd into a hart;
    And my desires, like fell and cruel hounds,
    E'er since pursue me.[4]—

[*Enter* VALENTINE.]

How now! what news from her?

---

[1] The sense of *dying*, as here used, is technically expressed by *diminuendo*.

[2] *Validity* is *worth, value*. So in *All's Well*, v. 3: "Behold this ring, whose high respect and rich *validity* did lack a parallel."

[3] *Fancy* is continually used by old writers for *love*. There is a play on the word here.

[4] Shakespeare seems to think men cautioned against too great familiarity with forbidden beauty by the fable of Actæon, who saw Diana naked, and was torn to pieces by his hounds; as a man indulging his eyes or his imagination with a view of a woman he cannot gain, has his heart torn with incessant longing.

VALENTINE. So please my lord, I might not be admitted,
 But from her handmaid do return this answer:
 The element[5] itself, till seven years' heat,
 Shall not behold her face at ample view;
 But like a cloistress she will veiled walk,
 And water once a-day her chamber round
 With eye-offending brine: all this to season[6]
 A brother's dead love, which she would keep fresh
 And lasting in her sad remembrance.
DUKE. O, she that hath a heart of that fine frame
 To pay this debt of love but to a brother,
 How will she love when the rich golden shaft
 Hath kill'd the flock of all affections else
 That live in her; when liver, brain, and heart,
 These sovereign thrones, are all supplied and fill'd,—
 Her sweet perfections,—with one self king![7]—
 Away before me to sweet beds of flowers:
 Love-thoughts lie rich when canopied with bowers. [*Exeunt.*]

SCENE II.

The Sea-Coast.

[*Enter* VIOLA, CAPTAIN, *and* SAILORS.]

VIOLA. What country, friends, is this?
CAPTAIN. This is Illyria, lady.
VIOLA. And what should I do in Illyria?
 My brother he is in Elysium.
 Perchance he is not drown'd—What think you, sailors?
CAPTAIN. It is perchance[8] that you yourself were sav'd.
VIOLA. O my poor brother! and so perchance may he be.
CAPTAIN. True, madam; and, to comfort you with chance,
 Assure yourself, after our ship did split,
 When you, and those poor number sav'd with you,

---

[5] *Element* here means the *sky*. So in *Henry IV., Part 2*, iv. 3: "And I, in the clear sky of fame, o'ershine you as much as the full Moon doth the cinders of the *element*, which show like pins' heads to her"; cinders meaning, of course, the *stars*.

[6] To *season* is to *preserve*. In *All's Well*, i. 1, tears are said to be "the best brine a maiden can *season* her praise in."

[7] The liver, brain, and heart were regarded as the special seats of passion, judgment, and affection, and so were put respectively for their supposed occupants.—*One self king* is equivalent to *one and the same king*. The Poet often uses *self* with the force of *salfsame*.

[8] Viola first uses *perchance* in the sense of *perhaps*; the Captain in that of *by chance, accident,* or *good luck.*

Hung on our driving boat,[9] I saw your brother,
Most provident in peril, bind himself,—
Courage and hope both teaching him the practice,—
To a strong mast that liv'd upon the sea;
Where, like Arion on the dolphin's back,[10]
I saw him hold acquaintance with the waves
So long as I could see.

VIOLA. [*giving him gold.*] For saying so, there's gold!
Mine own escape unfoldeth to my hope,
Whereto thy speech serves for authority,
The like of him. Know'st thou this country?

CAPTAIN. Ay, madam, well; for I was bred and born
Not three hours' travel from this very place.

VIOLA. Who governs here?

CAPTAIN. A noble duke, in nature as in name.[11]

VIOLA. What is his name?

CAPTAIN. Orsino.

VIOLA. Orsino! I have heard my father name him.
He was a bachelor then.

CAPTAIN. And so is now,
Or was so very late; for but a month
Ago I went from hence; and then 'twas fresh
In murmur,—as, you know, what great ones do,
The less will prattle of,—that he did seek
The love of fair Olivia.

VIOLA. What's she?

CAPTAIN. A virtuous maid, the daughter of a count
That died some twelvemonth since; then leaving her
In the protection of his son, her brother,
Who shortly also died; for whose dear love,

---

[9] "*Driving* boat" means, I suppose, boat *driven before the storm.*

[10] Arion's feat is worthily described in Wordsworth's poem *On the Power of sound*:

> Thy skill, Arion,
> Could humanize the creaures of the sea,
> Where men were monsters. A last grace he craves,
> Leave for one chant;—the dulcet sound
> Steals from the deck o'er willing waves,
> And listening dolphins gather round.
> Self-cast, as with a desperate course,
> Mid that strange audience, he bestrides
> A proud one docile as a managed horse;
> And singing, while the accordant hand
> Sweeps his harp, the master rides.

[11] An allusion, no doubt, to the great and well-known Italian family of *Orsini*, from whom the name *Orsino* is borrowed.

They say, she hath abjured the company
And sight of men.
VIOLA. O that I served that lady!
And might not be delivered to the world,
Till I had made mine own occasion mellow,
What my estate is![12]
CAPTAIN. That were hard to compass:
Because she will admit no kind of suit,
No, not the duke's.
VIOLA. There is a fair behaviour in thee, captain;
And though that nature with a beauteous wall
Doth oft close in pollution, yet of thee
I will believe thou hast a mind that suits
With this thy fair and outward character.
I pray thee, and I'll pay thee bounteously,
Conceal me what I am; and be my aid
For such disguise as, haply, shall become
The form of my intent. I'll serve this duke;
Thou shalt present me as an eunuch to him:[13]
It may be worth thy pains, for I can sing,
And speak to him in many sorts of music,
That will allow me very worth his service.[14]
What else may hap to time I will commit;
Only shape thou silence to my wit.
CAPTAIN. Be you his eunuch and your mute I'll be;
When my tongue blabs, then let mine eyes not see.
VIOLA. I thank thee. Lead me on. [*Exeunt.*]

SCENE III.

A Room in OLIVIA's *House.*

[*Enter* SIR TOBY BELCH *and* MARIA.]

SIR TOBY. What a plague means my niece, to take the death of her
brother thus? I am sure care's an enemy to life.

---

[12] Viola is herself a nobleman's daughter; and she here wishes that her birth and
quality—her *estate*—may he kept secret from the world, till she has a *ripe* occasion for
making known who she is. Certain later passages in the play seem to infer that she has
already fallen in love with Duke Orsino from the descriptions she has had of him.

[13] This plan of Viola's was not pursued, as it would have been inconsistent with the
plot of the play. She was presented as a *page*, not as a *eunuch*.

[14] "Will *approve* me worth his service"; that is, "will *prove* that *I am* worth," &c.
This use of to *allow* for to *approve* is very common in old English; and Shakespeare has
it repeatedly. So in *King Lear*, ii. 4: "O Heavens, if your sweet sway *allow* obedience."

MARIA. By my troth, Sir Toby, you must come in earlier o' nights; your cousin,[15] my lady, takes great exceptions to your ill hours.

SIR TOBY. Why, let her except, before excepted.[16]

MARIA. Ay, but you must confine yourself within the modest limits of order.

SIR TOBY. Confine? I'll confine myself no finer than I am:[17] these clothes are good enough to drink in, and so be these boots too; an they be not, let them hang themselves in their own straps.

MARIA. That quaffing and drinking will undo you: I heard my lady talk of it yesterday; and of a foolish knight that you brought in one night here to be her wooer.

SIR TOBY. Who? Sir Andrew Aguecheek?

MARIA. Ay, he.

SIR TOBY. He's as tall a man[18] as any's in Illyria.

MARIA. What's that to the purpose?

SIR TOBY. Why, he has three thousand ducats a year.

MARIA. Ay, but he'll have but a year in all these ducats; he's a very fool, and a prodigal.

SIR TOBY. Fye that you'll say so! he plays o' the viol-de-gamboys,[19] and speaks three or four languages word for word without book, and hath all the good gifts of nature.

MARIA. He hath indeed,—almost natural:[20] for, besides that he's a fool, he's a great quarreller; and, but that he hath the gift of a coward to allay the gust[21] he hath in quarrelling, 'tis thought among the prudent he would quickly have the gift of a grave.

SIR TOBY. By this hand, they are scoundrels and subtractors[22] that say so of him. Who are they?

---

[15] *Cousin* was used, not only for what we so designate, but also for *nephew, niece, grandchild*, and, indeed, *kindred* in general.

[16] The Poet here shows his familiarity with the technical language of the Law; Sir Toby being made to run a whimsical play upon the old legal phrase, "those things being excepted which were before excepted."

[17] Sir Toby purposely misunderstands *confine*, taking it for *refine*.

[18] The use of *tall* for *bold, valiant, stout*, was common in Shakespeare's time, and occurs several times in his works. Sir Toby is evidently bantering with the word, Sir Andrew being equally deficient in spirit and in stature.

[19] *Viol-de-gamboys* appears to be a Tobyism for *viol da gamba*, an instrument much like the violoncello: so called because it was held between the legs; *gamba* being Italian for *leg*. According to Gifford, the instrument "was an indispensable piece of furniture in every fashionable house, where it hung up in the best chamber, much as the guitar does in Spain, and the violin in Italy, to be played on at will, and to fill up the void of conversation. Whoever pretended to fashion affected an acquaintance with this instrument."

[20] Maria plays upon *natural*, which, in one of its senses, meant a *fool.*—There is also an equivoque in *all most*, one of the senses being *almost*.

[21] *Gust* is *taste*, from the Italian *gusto*; not much used now, though its sense lives in *disgust*.

[22] *Subtractors* is another Tobyism for *detractors*.

MARIA. They that add, moreover, he's drunk nightly in your company.

SIR TOBY. With drinking healths to my niece; I'll drink to her as long as there is a passage in my throat and drink in Illyria. He's a coward and a coistrel[23] that will not drink to my niece till his brains turn o' the toe like a parish-top.[24] What, wench! *Castiliano vulto*;[25] for here comes Sir Andrew Ague-face.

[*Enter* SIR ANDREW AGUECHEEK.]

SIR ANDREW. Sir Toby Belch! how now, Sir Toby Belch!

SIR TOBY. Sweet Sir Andrew?

SIR ANDREW. Bless you, fair shrew.

MARIA. And you too, sir.

SIR TOBY. Accost, Sir Andrew, accost.[26]

SIR ANDREW. What's that?

SIR TOBY. My niece's chamber-maid.

SIR ANDREW. Good Mistress Accost, I desire better acquaintance.

MARIA. My name is Mary, sir.

SIR ANDREW. Good Mistress Mary Accost,—

SIR TOBY. You mistake, knight: *accost* is, front her, board her, woo her, assail her.

SIR ANDREW. By my troth, I would not undertake her in this company. Is that the meaning of *accost*?

MARIA. Fare you well, gentlemen.

SIR TOBY. An thou let part so,[27] Sir Andrew, would thou mightst never draw sword again.

SIR ANDREW. An you part so, mistress, I would I might never draw sword again. Fair lady, do you think you have fools in hand?

MARIA. Sir, I have not you by the hand.

SIR ANDREW. Marry, but you shall have; and here's my hand.

MARIA. Now, sir, thought is free. I pray you, bring your hand to the buttery-bar and let it drink.[28]

SIR ANDREW. Wherefore, sweetheart? what's your metaphor?

---

[23] Holinshed classes *coistrels* among the unwarlike followers of an army. It was thus used as a term of contempt.

[24] A large top was formerly kept in each village for the peasantry to amuse themselves with in frosty weather. "He sleeps like a town-top," is an old proverb.

[25] Meaning, "Put on a Castilian face"; that is, grave, solemn looks.

[26] Sir Toby speaks more learnedly than intelligibly here, using *accost* in its original sense. The word is from the French *accoster*, to come *side by side*, or to *approach*, *Accost* is seldom used thus, which accounts for Sir Andrew's mistake.

[27] *Part* for *depart*. A frequent usage.

[28] The *buttery* was formerly a place for all sorts of gastric refreshments, and a dry hand was considered a symptom of debility.—The relevancy of "thought is free" may be not very apparent. Perhaps the following from Lyly's *Euphues*, 1581, will illustrate it: "None, quoth she, can judge of wit but they that have it. Why, then, quoth he, dost thou think me a fool? *Thought is free*, my lord, quoth she."

MARIA. It's dry, sir.

SIR ANDREW. Why, I think so; I am not such an ass but I can keep my hand dry. But what's your jest?

MARIA. A dry jest, sir.

SIR ANDREW. Are you full of them?

MARIA. Ay, sir, I have them at my fingers' ends: marry, now I let go your hand I am barren. [*Exit.*]

SIR TOBY. O knight, thou lack'st a cup of canary: When did I see thee so put down?

SIR ANDREW. Never in your life, I think; unless you see canary put me down. Methinks sometimes I have no more wit than a Christian or an ordinary man has; but I am great eater of beef, and, I believe, that does harm to my wit.[29]

SIR TOBY. No question.

SIR ANDREW. An I thought that, I'd forswear it. I'll ride home to-morrow, Sir Toby.

SIR TOBY. *Pourquoi*, my dear knight?

SIR ANDREW. What is *pourquoi*? do or not do? I would I had bestowed that time in the tongues that I have in fencing, dancing, and bear-baiting. Oh, had I but followed the arts!

SIR TOBY. Then hadst thou had an excellent head of hair.[30]

SIR ANDREW. Why, would that have mended my hair?

SIR TOBY. Past question; for thou seest it will not curl by nature.

SIR ANDREW. But it becomes me well enough, does't not?

SIR TOBY. Excellent; it hangs like flax on a distaff; and I hope to see a housewife take thee between her legs and spin it off.

SIR ANDREW. Faith, I'll home to-morrow, Sir Toby; your niece will not be seen; or, if she be, it's four to one she'll none of me; the Count[31] himself here hard by woos her.

SIR TOBY. She'll none o' the Count; she'll not match above her degree, neither in estate, years, nor wit; I have heard her swear't. Tut, there's life in't,[32] man.

---

[29] So in *The Haven of Health*, 1584: "Galen affirmeth that biefe maketh grosse bloude and engendreth melancholie, especially if it is much eaten, and if such as doe eat it be of a melancholy complexion."

[30] Sir Toby is quibbling between *tongues* and *tongs*, the latter meaning, of course, the well-known instrument for *curling* the hair. The two words were often written, and probably sounded, alike, or nearly so. So in the introduction to *The Faerie Queene*: "O, helpe thou my weake wit, and sharpen my dull *tong*." Here the word rhymes with *long* and *wrong*. For this explanation, which is not more ingenious than apt and just, I am indebted to a private letter from Mr. Joseph Crosby.

[31] The titles *Duke* and *Count* are used indifferently of Orsino. The reason of this, if there be any, is not apparent. The Poet of course understood the difference between a duke and a count, well enough. White suggests that in a. revisal of the play he may have concluded to change the title, and then, for some cause, left the change incomplete.

[32] Equivalent to "there is *hope* in it." It was a phrase of the time.

SIR ANDREW. I'll stay a month longer. I am a fellow o' the strangest mind i' the world; I delight in masques and revels sometimes altogether.

SIR TOBY. Art thou good at these kickshawes,[33] knight?

SIR ANDREW. As any man in Illyria, whatsoever he be, under the degree of my betters; and yet I will not compare with an old man.

SIR TOBY. What is thy excellence in a galliard, knight?

SIR ANDREW. Faith, I can cut a caper.

SIR TOBY. And I can cut the mutton to't.[34]

SIR ANDREW. And, I think, I have the back-trick simply as strong as any man in Illyria.

SIR TOBY. Wherefore are these things hid? wherefore have these gifts a curtain before them? are they like to take dust, like Mistress Mall's picture?[35] why dost thou not go to church in a galliard and come home in a coranto?[36] My very walk should be a jig; I would not so much as make water but in a sink-a-pace.[37] What dost thou mean? is it a world to hide virtues in? I did think, by the excellent constitution of thy leg, it was formed under the star of a galliard.

SIR ANDREW. Ay, 'tis strong, and it does indifferent well in flame-colour'd stock.[38] Shall we set about some revels?

SIR TOBY. What shall we do else? were we not born under Taurus?

SIR ANDREW. Taurus? that's sides and heart.

SIR TOBY. No, sir; it is legs and thighs.[39] Let me see thee caper. [SIR ANDREW *dances.*] Ha, higher: ha, ha!—excellent! [*Exeunt.*]

---

[33] A Tobyism, probably, for *kickshaws*, an old word for *trifles* or *knick-knacks*; said to be a corruption of the French *quelque chose*.

[34] A double pun is probably intended here; the meaning being, "If you can do the man's part in a galliard, I can do the woman's." *Mutton* was sometimes used as a slang term for a *woman*.

[35] *Mistress Mall* was a very celebrated character of the Poet's time, who played many parts (not on the stage) in male attire. Her real name was Mary Frith, though commonly known as Moll Cutpurse. In 1610 a book was entered at the Stationers, called *The Madde Prankes of Merry Moll of the Bankside, with her Walks in Man's Apparel, and to what purpose,* by John Day. Middleton and Dekker wrote a comedy entitled *The Roaring Girl,* of which she was the heroine. Portraits were commonly curtained to keep off the dust.

[36] *Galliard* and *coranto* are names of dances: the galliard, a lively, stirring dance, from a Spanish word signifying cheerful, gay; the coranto, a quick dance for two persons, described as "traversing and running, as our country dance, but having twice as much in a strain."

[37] *Sink-a-pace* was a popular corruption of *cinque-pace*; a dance, the steps of which were regulated by the number five.

[38] "A flame-colour'd *stock*" is a pretty emphatic sort of stocking.—"*Indifferent* well" is *tolerably* well. A frequent usage.

[39] Alluding to the medical astrology of the almanacs. Both the knights are wrong; the zodiacal sign Taurus having reference to the neck and throat. The point seems to be that Sir Toby is poking fun at Sir Andrew's conceit of agility: "I can cut a caper."

SCENE IV.

A Room in the DUKE'*s Palace.*

[*Enter* VALENTINE, *and* VIOLA *in man's attire.*]

VALENTINE. If the Duke continue these favours towards you,
Cesario, you are like to be much advanced; he hath known you but
three days, and already you are no stranger.
VIOLA. You either fear his humour or my negligence, that you call in
question the continuance of his love. Is he inconstant, sir, in his
favours?
VALENTINE. No, believe me.

[*Enter* DUKE, CURIO, *and* ATTENDANTS.]

VIOLA. I thank you. Here comes the count.
DUKE. Who saw Cesario, ho?
VIOLA. On your attendance, my lord; here.
DUKE. [*to* CURIO *and* ATTENDANTS.] Stand you awhile aloof.—
    Cesario,
    Thou know'st no less but all;[40] I have unclasp'd
    To thee the book even of my secret soul:
    Therefore, good youth, address thy gait[41] unto her;
    Be not denied access, stand at her doors,
    And tell them there thy fixed foot shall grow
    Till thou have audience.
VIOLA. Sure, my noble lord,
    If she be so abandon'd to her sorrow
    As it is spoke, she never will admit me.
DUKE. Be clamorous and leap all civil bounds,
    Rather than make unprofited[42] return.
VIOLA. Say I do speak with her, my lord. What then?
DUKE. O, then unfold the passion of my love,
    Surprise her with discourse of my dear faith:
    It shall become thee well to act my woes;

---

[40] That is, "no less *than* all." This use of *but* with the force of *than* is quite frequent
in Shakespeare. In *As You Like It*, we have five instances of it in one speech: "Your
brother and my sister no sooner met, *but* they looked"; &c.

[41] The meaning is, "*direct* thy *course*," or thy *steps*. The Poet often uses to *address*
in the sense of to *make ready* or *prepare*; and here the meaning is much the same.

[42] *Unprofited* for *unprofitable*. Shakespeare often uses the endings -*able* and -*ed*
indiscriminately. So he has *detested* for *detestable*, *unnumbered* for *innumerable*,
unavoided for *unavoidable*, and many others.

She will attend it better in thy youth
Than in a nuncio of more grave aspect.
VIOLA. I think not so, my lord.
DUKE. Dear lad, believe it,
For they shall yet belie thy happy years
That say thou art a man: Diana's lip
Is not more smooth and rubious;[43] thy small pipe
Is as the maiden's organ, shrill and sound,
And all is semblative a woman's part.
I know thy constellation[44] is right apt
For this affair:—
[*to* CURIO and attendants.] some four or five attend him:
All, if you will; for I myself am best
When least in company:—[*to* VIOLA.] prosper well in this,
And thou shalt live as freely as thy lord,
To call his fortunes thine.
VIOLA. I'll do my best
To woo your lady:—[*Aside.*] Yet, a barful strife![45]
Whoe'er I woo, myself would be his wife.

SCENE V.

A Room in OLIVIA'*s House.*

[*Enter* MARIA *and* CLOWN.]

MARIA. Nay; either tell me where thou hast been, or I will not open
my lips so wide as a bristle may enter in way of thy excuse: my
lady will hang thee for thy absence.
CLOWN. Let her hang me: he that is well hanged in this world needs to
fear no colours.[46]
MARIA. Make that good.
CLOWN. He shall see none to fear.
MARIA. A good lenten answer.[47] I can tell thee where that saying was
born, of, *I fear no colours.*

---

[43] Rubious is *red* or *rosy.* This sense lives in *ruby* and *rubicund.*

[44] An astrological allusion. A man's constellation is the star that was in the ascendant at his birth, and so determined what he had a genius for.

[45] A strife or undertaking *full of bars* or *impediments.*

[46] Both the origin of this phrase and the meaning attached to it, notwithstanding Maria's explanation, are still obscure. *Colours* is still used for *flag;* and probably it is here to be taken in a figurative sense for *enemy.*

[47] Probably a *short* or *spare* answer; like the diet used in Lent. *Lenten* might be applied to any thing that marked the season of Lent. Thus Taylor the water-poet speaks of "a lenten top," which people amused themselves with during Lent; and in *Hamlet* we have, "what lenten entertainment the players shall receive from you."

CLOWN. Where, good Mistress Mary?

MARIA. In the wars; and that may you be bold to say in your foolery.

CLOWN. Well, God give them wisdom that have it; and those that are fools, let them use their talents.

MARIA. Yet you will be hanged for being so long absent: or to be turned away; is not that as good as a hanging to you?

CLOWN. Many a good hanging prevents a bad marriage; and for turning away, let summer bear it out.

MARIA. You are resolute, then?

CLOWN. Not so, neither: but I am resolved on two points.

MARIA. That if one break, the other will hold; or if both break, your gaskins fall.[48]

CLOWN. Apt, in good faith, very apt! Well, go thy way; if Sir Toby would leave drinking, thou wert as witty a piece of Eve's flesh as any in Illyria.

MARIA. Peace, you rogue; no more o' that; here comes my lady: make your excuse wisely; you were best. [*Exit.*]

CLOWN. Wit, and't be thy will, put me into good fooling! Those wits that think they have thee do very oft prove fools; and I, that am sure I lack thee, may pass for a wise man. For what says Quinapalus?[49] *Better a witty fool than a foolish wit.*—

[*Enter* OLIVIA *and* MALVOLIO.]

God bless thee, lady!

OLIVIA. Take the Fool away.

CLOWN. Do you not hear, fellows? Take away the lady.

OLIVIA. Go to, you're a dry fool; I'll no more of you: besides, you grow dishonest.

CLOWN. Two faults, madonna, that drink and good counsel will amend: for give the dry fool drink, then is the Fool not dry; bid the dishonest man mend himself: if he mend, he is no longer dishonest; if he cannot, let the botcher mend him. Anything that's mended is but patched; virtue that transgresses is but patched with sin, and sin that amends is but patched with virtue. If that this simple syllogism will serve, so; if it will not, what remedy? As there is no true cuckold but calamity, so beauty's a flower:—the lady bade take away the Fool; therefore, I say again, take her away.

OLIVIA. Sir, I bade them take away you.

CLOWN. Misprision in the highest degree!—Lady, *Cucullus non facit monachum*;[50] that's as much to say, I wear not motley in my brain. Good madonna, give me leave to prove you a fool.

OLIVIA. Can you do it?

CLOWN. Dexteriously, good madonna.

OLIVIA. Make your proof.

CLOWN. I must catechize you for it, madonna. Good my mouse of virtue, answer me.

OLIVIA. Well, sir, for want of other idleness, I'll 'bide your proof.

CLOWN. Good madonna, why mourn'st thou?

OLIVIA. Good fool, for my brother's death.

CLOWN. I think his soul is in Hell, madonna.

OLIVIA. I know his soul is in Heaven, fool.

CLOWN. The more fool you, madonna, to mourn for your brother's soul being in Heaven.—Take away the Fool, gentlemen.

OLIVIA. What think you of this fool, Malvolio? doth he not mend?

MALVOLIO. Yes; and shall do, till the pangs of death shake him. Infirmity, that decays the wise, doth ever make the better fool.

CLOWN. God send you, sir, a speedy infirmity, for the better increasing your folly! Sir Toby will be sworn that I am no fox; but he will not pass his word for twopence that you are no fool.

OLIVIA. How say you to that, Malvolio?

MALVOLIO. I marvel your ladyship takes delight in such a barren rascal; I saw him put down the other day with an ordinary fool that has no more brain than a stone. Look you now, he's out of his guard already; unless you laugh and minister occasion to him, he is gagged. I protest I take these wise men that crow so at these set kind of fools, no better than the Fools' zanies.[51]

OLIVIA. O, you are sick of self-love, Malvolio, and taste with a distempered appetite. To be generous, guiltless, and of free disposition, is to take those things for bird-bolts[52] that you deem

---

[50] A common proverb; literally, "a hood does not make a monk." Shakespeare has it elsewhere.

[51] The *zany* in Shakespeare's day was the attenuated mime of the mimic. He was the servant or attendant of the professional clown, who accompanied him on the stage or in the ring, attempting to imitate his tricks, and adding to the general merriment by his ludicrous failures and comic imbecility. It is this characteristic, not merely of mimicry, but of weak and abortive mimicry, that gives its distinctive meaning to the word, and colours it with a special tinge of contempt. This feature of the early stage has descended to our own times, and may still be found in the performances of the circus. We have ourselves seen the clown and the zany in the ring together; the clown doing clever tricks, the zany provoking immense laughter by his ludicrous failures in attempting to imitate them.—*Edinburgh Review*, July, 1869.

[52] *Bird-bolts* were short thick arrows with obtuse ends, used for shooting young rocks and other birds.

cannon bullets. There is no slander in an allowed Fool,[53] though he do nothing but rail; nor no railing in known discreet man, though he do nothing but reprove.

CLOWN. Now Mercury endue thee with leasing,[54] for thou speakest well of fools!

[*Re-enter* MARIA.]

MARIA. Madam, there is at the gate a young gentleman much desires to speak with you.

OLIVIA. From the Count Orsino, is it?

MARIA. I know not, madam; 'tis a fair young man, and well attended.

OLIVIA. Who of my people hold him in delay?

MARIA. Sir Toby, madam, your kinsman.

OLIVIA. Fetch him off, I pray you; he speaks nothing but madman. Fie on him! [*Exit* MARIA.]—Go you, Malvolio: if it be a suit from the count, I am sick, or not at home; what you will to dismiss it. [*Exit* MALVOLIO.]—Now you see, sir, how your fooling grows old, and people dislike it.

CLOWN. Thou hast spoke for us, madonna, as if thy eldest son should be a fool: whose skull Jove cram with brains, for here he comes— one of thy kin, has a most weak *pia mater*.[55]

[*Enter* SIR TOBY BELCH.]

OLIVIA. By mine honour, half drunk!—What is he at the gate, cousin?

SIR TOBY. A gentleman.

OLIVIA. A gentleman? What gentleman?

SIR TOBY. 'Tis a gentleman here.—a plague o' these pickle-herrings![56]—How now, sot![57]

CLOWN. Good Sir Toby!—

OLIVIA. Cousin, cousin, how have you come so early by this lethargy?

SIR TOBY. Lechery! I defy[58] lechery. There's one at the gate.

---

[53] An *allow'd Fool* was the domestic or court Fool, like Touchstone in *As You Like It*; that is, the jester by profession, who dressed in motley; with whom folly was an art; and whose functions are so admirably set forth by Jaques in the play just mentioned, ii. 7.

[54] The Clown means, that unless Olivia *lied* she could not "speak well of Fools"; therefore he prays Mercury to endue her with *leasing*. *Leasing* was about the same as our *fibbing*. As Mercury was the God of cheats and liars, the Clown aptly invokes his aid.

[55] The membrane that covers the brain; put for the brain itself.

[56] Pickled herrings seem to have been a common relish in drunken sprees. Gabriel Harvey says of Robert Greene, the profligate dramatist, that he died "of a surfett of pickle herringe and Rennishe wine."

[57] *Sot* is used by the Poet for *fool*; as in *The Merry Wives* Dr. Caius says, "Have you make-a de *sot* of us?"

[58] To *defy* was often used for to *renounce*, or *abjure*.

OLIVIA. Ay, marry; what is he?

SIR TOBY. Let him be the Devil an he will, I care not: give me faith, say I. Well, it's all one. [*Exit.*]

OLIVIA. What's a drunken man like, fool?

CLOWN. Like a drowned man, a fool, and a madman: one draught above heat makes him a fool; the second mads him; and a third drowns him.

OLIVIA. Go thou and seek the coroner, and let him sit o' my coz; for he's in the third degree of drink;—he's drowned: go, look after him.

CLOWN. He is but mad yet, madonna; and the Fool shall look to the madman. [*Exit.*]

[*Re-enter* MALVOLIO.]

MALVOLIO. Madam, yond young fellow swears he will speak with you. I told him you were sick; he takes on him to understand so much, and therefore comes to speak with you; I told him you were asleep; he seems to have a foreknowledge of that too, and therefore comes to speak with you. What is to be said to him, lady? he's fortified against any denial.

OLIVIA. Tell him, he shall not speak with me.

MALVOLIO. Has been told so; and he says he'll stand at your door like a sheriff's post,[59] and be the supporter of a bench, but he'll speak with you.

OLIVIA. What kind of man is he?

MALVOLIO. Why, of mankind.

OLIVIA. What manner of man?

MALVOLIO. Of very ill manner; he'll speak with you, will you or no.

OLIVIA. Of what personage and years is he?

MALVOLIO. Not yet old enough for a man, nor young enough for a boy; as a squash is before 'tis a peascod, or a codling, when 'tis almost an apple:[60] 'tis with him e'en standing water, between boy and man. He is very well-favoured, and he speaks very shrewishly;[61] one would think his mother's milk were scarce out of him.

OLIVIA. Let him approach. Call in my gentlewoman.

---

[59] The Sheriffs formerly had painted posts set up at their doors on which proclamations and placards were affixed.

[60] A *codling*, according to Gifford, means an *involucrum* or *kell*, and was used by our old writers for that early stage of vegetation, when the fruit, after shaking off the blossom, begins to assume a globular and determinate shape. The original of *squash* was used of such young vegetables as were eaten in the state of immaturity.

[61] *Shrewishly* is *sharply*, *tartly*; like a *shrew*. So, of old, *shrewd* meant *keen* or *biting*.

MALVOLIO. Gentlewoman, my lady calls. [*Exit.*]

[*Re-enter* MARIA.]

OLIVIA. Give me my veil; come, throw it o'er my face;
We'll once more hear Orsino's embassy.

[*Enter* VIOLA.]

VIOLA. The honourable lady of the house, which is she?
OLIVIA. Speak to me; I shall answer for her. Your will?
VIOLA. Most radiant, exquisite, and unmatchable beauty,—I pray you,
tell me if this be the lady of the house, for I never saw her: I would
be loath to cast away my speech; for, besides that it is excellently
well penned, I have taken great pains to con it. Good beauties, let
me sustain no scorn; I am very comptible[62] even to the least
sinister usage.
OLIVIA. Whence came you, sir?
VIOLA. I can say little more than I have studied, and that question's
out of my part. Good gentle one, give me modest assurance, if you
be the lady of the house, that I may proceed in my speech.
OLIVIA. Are you a comedian?
VIOLA. No, my profound heart: and yet, by the very fangs of malice I
swear, I am not that I play. Are you the lady of the house?
OLIVIA. If I do not usurp myself, I am.
VIOLA. Most certain, if you are she, you do usurp yourself; for what is
yours to bestow is not yours to reserve. But this is from my
commission: I will on with my speech in your praise, and then
show you the heart of my message.
OLIVIA. Come to what is important in't: I forgive you the praise.
VIOLA. Alas, I took great pains to study it, and 'tis poetical.
OLIVIA. It is the more like to be feigned; I pray you keep it in. I heard
you were saucy at my gates; and allowed your approach, rather to
wonder at you than to hear you. If you be not mad, be gone; if you
have reason, be brief: 'tis not that time of moon with me to make
one in so skipping a dialogue.
MARIA. Will you hoist sail, sir? here lies your way.
VIOLA. No, good swabber; I am to hull here[63] a little longer.—Some
mollification for your giant,[64] sweet lady.

---

[62] *Comptible* is *susceptible*, or *sensitive*. The proper meaning of the word is
accountable.

[63] To *hull* is a nautical term, probably meaning to haul in sails and layto, without
coming to anchor. *Swabber* is also a nautical term, used of one who attends td the
swabbing or cleaning of the deck.

OLIVIA. Tell me your mind.

VIOLA. I am a messenger.[65]

OLIVIA. Sure, you have some hideous matter to deliver, when the courtesy of it is so fearful. Speak your office.

VIOLA. It alone concerns your ear. I bring no overture of war, no taxation of homage; I hold the olive in my hand: my words are as full of peace as matter.

OLIVIA. Yet you began rudely. What are you? what would you?

VIOLA. The rudeness that hath appeared in me have I learned from my entertainment. What I am and what I would are as secret as maidenhead: to your ears, divinity; to any other's, profanation.

OLIVIA. Give us the place alone: we will hear this divinity. [*Exit* MARIA.]—Now, sir, what is your text?

VIOLA. Most sweet lady,—

OLIVIA. A comfortable[66] doctrine, and much may be said of it. Where lies your text?

VIOLA. In Orsino's bosom.

OLIVIA. In his bosom? In what chapter of his bosom?

VIOLA. To answer by the method, in the first of his heart.

OLIVIA. O, I have read it; it is heresy. Have you no more to say?

VIOLA. Good madam, let me see your face.

OLIVIA. Have you any commission from your lord to negotiate with my face? you are now out of your text: but we will draw the curtain and show you the picture. Look you, sir, such a one I was this present:[67] Is't not well done?

[*Unveiling.*]

VIOLA. Excellently done, if God did all.

OLIVIA. 'Tis in grain, sir; 'twill endure wind and weather.

VIOLA. 'Tis beauty truly blent, whose red and white
Nature's own sweet and cunning hand laid on:
Lady, you are the cruel'st she alive,
If you will lead these graces to the grave,
And leave the world no copy.

OLIVIA. O, sir, I will not be so hard-hearted; I will give out divers schedules of my beauty. It shall be inventoried; and every particle

---

[64] Ladies in romance are guarded by giants. Viola, seeing the waiting-maid so eager to oppose her message, entreats Olivia to pacify her giant, alluding, ironically, to the small stature of Maria.

[65] Viola's being a messenger implies that it is not her own mind, but that of the sender, that she is to tell.

[66] *Comfortable* for *comforting*; the passive form with the active sense. Often so.

[67] It is to be borne in mind that the idea of a picture is continued; the meaning being, "behold the picture of me, such as I am at the present moment."

and utensil labelled to my will: as, item, two lips indifferent red;[68]
item, two gray eyes,[69] with lids to them; item, one neck, one chin,
and so forth. Were you sent hither to 'praise me?[70]

VIOLA. I see you what you are,—you are too proud;
But, if you were the Devil, you are fair.
My lord and master loves you. O, such love
Could be but recompens'd though you were crown'd
The nonpareil of beauty!

OLIVIA. How does he love me?

VIOLA. With adorations, fertile tears,[71]
With groans that thunder love, with sighs of fire.

OLIVIA. Your lord does know my mind; I cannot love him:
Yet I suppose him virtuous, know him noble,
Of great estate, of fresh and stainless youth;
In voices well divulged,[72] free, learn'd, and valiant,
And, in dimension and the shape of nature,
A gracious person: but yet I cannot love him;
He might have took his answer long ago.

VIOLA. If I did love you in my master's flame,
With such a suffering, such a deadly life,
In your denial I would find no sense,
I would not understand it.

OLIVIA. Why, what would you?

VIOLA. Make me a willow cabin at your gate,
And call upon my soul within the house;
Write loyal cantons[73] of contemned love,
And sing them loud, even in the dead of night;
Holla your name to the reverberate hills,
And make the babbling gossip of the air[74]
Cry out *Olivia*! O, you should not rest
Between the elements of air and earth,
But you should pity me!

OLIVIA. You might do much. What is your parentage?

VIOLA. Above my fortunes, yet my state is well: I am a gentleman.

OLIVIA. Get you to your lord;

---

[68] "*Indifferent* red" is *tolerably* red.

[69] *Blue* eyes were called *gray* in the Poet's time.

[70] To *appraise* me, or *set a value upon* me; referring to the *inventory* she has just given of her graces.

[71] *Fertile* appears to be used here in the sense of *copious*. Shakespeare has *fruitful* in a like sense. So in *Hamlet*, i. 2: "No, nor the *fruitful* river in the eye."

[72] Meaning, perhaps, well-spoken of, well *voiced* in the public mouth; or it may mean well reputed for knowledge in the languages, which was esteemed a great accomplishment in the Poet's time.

[73] *Cantons* is the old English word for *cantos*.

[74] A Shakespearian expression for *echo*.

I cannot love him: let him send no more;
Unless, perchance, you come to me again,
To tell me how he takes it. Fare you well:
I thank you for your pains: spend this for me.
VIOLA. I am no fee'd post, lady; keep your purse;
My master, not myself, lacks recompense.
Love make his heart of flint that you shall love;
And let your fervour, like my master's, be
Placed in contempt! Farewell, fair cruelty. [*Exit.*]
OLIVIA. *What is your parentage?*—
Above my fortunes, yet my state is well:
I am a gentleman.—I'll be sworn thou art;
Thy tongue, thy face, thy limbs, actions, and spirit,
Do give thee five-fold blazon. Not too fast:—
Soft, soft!—[75]
Unless the master were the man.—How now?
Even so quickly may one catch the plague?
Methinks I feel this youth's perfections
With an invisible and subtle stealth
To creep in at mine eyes. Well, let it be.—
What, ho, Malvolio!—

[*Re-enter* MALVOLIO.]

MALVOLIO. Here, madam, at your service.
OLIVIA. Run after that same peevish[76] messenger,
The county's man: he left this ring behind him,
Would I or not; tell him I'll none of it.
Desire him not to flatter with his lord,
Nor hold him up with hopes; I am not for him:
If that the youth will come this way to-morrow,
I'll give him reasons for't. Hie thee, Malvolio.
MALVOLIO. Madam, I will. [*Exit.*]
OLIVIA. I do I know not what: and fear to find
Mine eye too great a flatterer for my mind.[77]
Fate, show thy force. Ourselves we do not owe;[78]
What is decreed must be,—and be this so! [*Exit.*]

---

[75] *Soft*! was in frequent use, as here, for *stay*! *not too fast*! Olivia means, apparently, that her passion is going ahead too fast, unless Orsino were its object, who is Viola's *master*.

[76] *Peevish* was commonly used for *foolish* or *childish*; hence, perhaps, the meaning it now bears of *fretful*. It may have either meaning here, or both.

[77] She fears that her eyes have formed so flattering an idea of Cesario, that she will not have the strength of mind to resist the impression.

[78] We are not our own masters; we cannot govern ourselves. *Owe* for *own*, *possess*, or *have*; as usual.

ACT II.

SCENE I.

The Sea-coast.

[*Enter* ANTONIO *and* SEBASTIAN.]

ANTONIO. Will you stay no longer; nor will you not that I go with you?

SEBASTIAN. By your patience, no; my stars shine darkly over me; the malignancy of my fate might, perhaps, distemper yours; therefore I shall crave of you your leave that I may bear my evils alone. It were a bad recompense for your love, to lay any of them on you.

ANTONIO. Let me know of you whither you are bound.

SEBASTIAN. No, sooth, sir; my determinate voyage is mere extravagancy.[79] But I perceive in you so excellent a touch of modesty, that you will not extort from me what I am willing[80] to keep in; therefore it charges me in manners the rather to express myself.[81] You must know of me then, Antonio, my name is Sebastian, which I called Roderigo; my father was that Sebastian of Messaline whom I know you have heard of: he left behind him myself and a sister, both born in an hour; if the heavens had been pleased, would we had so ended! but you, sir, altered that; for some hours before you took me from the breach of the sea was my sister drowned.

ANTONIO. Alas the day!

SEBASTIAN. A lady, sir, though it was said she much resembled me, was yet of many accounted beautiful: but though I could not, with such estimable wonder, over-far believe that,[82] yet thus far I will boldly publish her,—she bore mind that envy could not but call fair. She is drowned already, sir, with salt water, though I seem to drown her remembrance again with more.

ANTONIO. Pardon me, sir, your bad entertainment.

SEBASTIAN. O, good Antonio, forgive me your trouble.

---

[79] "The purpose of my voyage ends with the voyage itself," or, "I am travelling merely for the sake of travel." *Extravagancy* is used in the Latin sense of going at large; as in *Hamlet*, i. 1: "Th' *extravagant* and erring spirit hies to his confine."

[80] *Willing* in the sense of *choosing, wishing,* or *preferring.*

[81] To declare or unfold myself. Sebastian holds' himself the more bound to give the information, inasmuch as Antonio's delicacy keeps him from asking, or from being inquisitive.

[82] The meaning is, "Though I could not, when compared with a person of such admirable beauty, over-far believe that I resembled her."

ANTONIO. If you will not murder me for my love,[83] let me be your
    servant.

SEBASTIAN. If you will not undo what you have done—that is, kill
    him whom you have recovered—desire it not. Fare ye well at once;
    my bosom is full of kindness; and I am yet so near the manners of
    my mother that, upon the least occasion more, mine eyes will tell
    tales of me. I am bound to the Count Orsino's court: farewell.
    [*Exit.*]

ANTONIO. The gentleness of all the gods go with thee!
    I have many enemies in Orsino's court,
    Else would I very shortly see thee there:
    But come what may, I do adore thee so
    That danger shall seem sport, and I will go. [*Exit.*]

SCENE II.

A Street.

[*Enter* VIOLA; MALVOLIO *following.*]

MALVOLIO. Were you not even now with the Countess Olivia?

VIOLA. Even now, sir; on a moderate pace I have since arrived but
    hither.

MALVOLIO. She returns this ring to you, sir; you might have saved
    me my pains, to have taken it away yourself. She adds moreover,
    that you should put your lord into a desperate assurance she will
    none of him: and one thing more: that you be never so hardy to
    come again in his affairs, unless it be to report your lord's taking of
    this. Receive it so.[84]

VIOLA. She took the ring of me: I'll none of it.

MALVOLIO. Come, sir, you peevishly threw it to her; and her will is it
    should be so returned. If it be worth stooping for, there it lies in
    your eye; if not, be it his that finds it. [*Exit.*]

VIOLA. I left no ring with her; what means this lady?
    Fortune forbid my outside have not charm'd her!
    She made good view of me; indeed, so much,

---

    [83] This may refer to what is thus delivered by Sir Walter Scott in *The Pirate*: When
Mordaunt has rescued Cleveland from the sea, and is trying to revive him, Bryce the
pedler says to him,—"Are you mad? you, that have so long lived in Zetland, to risk the
saving of a drowning man ? Wot ye not, if you bring him to life again, he will be sure to
do you some capital injury?" Sir Walter suggests in a note that this inhuman maxim was
probably held by the islanders of the Orkneys, as an excuse for leaving all to perish alone
who were shipwrecked upon their coasts, to the end that there might be nothing to hinder
the plundering of their goods; which of course could not well be, if any of the owners
survived.

    [84] "*Receive* it so" is *understand* it so. *Take* is still used in the same way.

That methought her eyes had lost her tongue,[85]
For she did speak in starts distractedly.
She loves me, sure: the cunning of her passion
Invites me in this churlish messenger.
None of my lord's ring! why, he sent her none.
I am the man;—if it be so,—as 'tis,—
Poor lady, she were better love a dream.
Disguise, I see thou art a wickedness
Wherein the pregnant[86] enemy does much.
How easy is it for the proper-false[87]
In women's waxen hearts to set their forms!
Alas, our frailty is the cause, not we;
For such as we are made of, such we be.[88]
How will this fadge?[89] My master loves her dearly,
And I, poor monster,[90] fond as much on him;
And she, mistaken, seems to dote on me.
What will become of this? As I am man,
My state is desperate for my master's love;
As I am woman,—now, alas the day!—
What thriftless sighs shall poor Olivia breathe!
O time, thou must untangle this, not I;
It is too hard a knot for me t' untie! [*Exit.*]

SCENE III.

A Room in OLIVIA'*s House.*

[*Enter* SIR TOBY BELCH *and* SIR ANDREW AGUECHEEK.]

SIR TOBY. Approach, Sir Andrew; not to be a-bed after midnight is to
be up betimes; and *diliculo surgere*,[91] thou know'st.

---

[85] Her eyes were so charmed that she lost the right use of her tongue, and let it run as if it were divided from her judgment.

[86] *Pregnant* is *quick-wilted, cunning.*

[87] *Proper* is here used in the sense of *handsome*: the meaning of the passage being, "How easy it is for handsome deceivers to print their forms in the waxen hearts of women." Such compounds as *proper-false* are not unusual in Shakespeare. *Beauteous-evil* occurs in this play.

[88] *Such* evidently refers to *frailty* in the preceding line; the sense being, "Since we are made of frailty, we must needs be frail."

[89] *Fadge*, meaning *fit* or *suit*, was a polite word in Shakespeare's time, and moved, without question, in the best circles.

[90] Viola calls herself *monster* from the fact of her being, in a manner, both woman and man.

[91] *Diliculo surgere, saluberrimum est.* This adage is in Lily's Grammar. It means, "To rise betimes is very wholesome."

SIR ANDREW. Nay; by my troth, I know not; but I know to be up late is to be up late.

SIR TOBY. A false conclusion; I hate it as an unfilled can. To be up after midnight, and to go to bed then is early: so that to go to bed after midnight is to go to bed betimes. Do not our lives consist of the four elements?[92]

SIR ANDREW. Faith, so they say; but I think it rather consists of eating and drinking.

SIR TOBY. Thou art a scholar; let us therefore eat and drink.—Marian, I say!—a stoup[93] of wine.

SIR ANDREW. Here comes the Fool, i'faith.

[*Enter* CLOWN.]

CLOWN. How now, my hearts? Did you never see the picture of *We Three*?[94]

SIR TOBY. Welcome, ass. Now let's have a catch.

SIR ANDREW. By my troth, the Fool has an excellent breast.[95] I had rather than forty shillings I had such a leg; and so sweet a breath to sing, as the Fool has.—In sooth, thou wast in very gracious fooling last night when thou spokest of Pigrogromitus, of the Vapians passing the equinoctial of Queubus; 'twas very good, i'faith. I sent thee sixpence for thy leman:[96] hadst it?

CLOWN. I did impeticos thy gratility;[97] for Malvolio's nose is no whipstock. My lady has a white hand, and the Myrmidons are no bottle-ale houses.

SIR ANDREW. Excellent! Why, this is the best fooling, when all is done. Now, a song.

SIR TOBY. Come on; there is sixpence for you: let's have a song.

SIR ANDREW. There's a testril[98] of me too: if one knight give a—

CLOWN. Would you have a love-song, or a song of good life?[99]

---

[92] The four elements referred to are earth, water, air, and fire; the right mixing of which was suposed to be the condition of health in body and mind.

[93] *Stoup* is an old word for *cup*; often used by the Poet.

[94] Alluding to an old common sign representing *two* fools or loggerheads, under which was inscribed, "We three loggerheads be"; the point of the joke being, of course, that the *spectator was the third.*

[95] *Breast* was often used for *voice* in the Poet's time. Thus we have the phrase, "singing men *well-breasted.*" This use of the word grew from the form of the breast having much to do with the quality of the voice.

[96] *Leman* is *mistress* or *sweetheart.*

[97] *Impetticoat,* or *impocket,* thy *gratuity.* Some have complained seriously that they could not understand the Clown in this scene; which is shrewd proof they did not understand the *Poet!*

[98] The *testril* or *testern* was originally a French coin, of sixpence value, or thereabouts; so called from having a *teste* or head stamped upon it.

SIR TOBY. A love-song, a love-song.
SIR ANDREW. Ay, ay; I care not for good life.
CLOWN.

SONG.[100]

> *O, mistress mine, where are you roaming?*
> *O, stay and hear; your true love's coming,*
>   *That can sing both high and low:*
> *Trip no further, pretty sweeting;*
> *Journeys end in lovers meeting,*
>   *Every wise man's son doth know.*

SIR ANDREW. Excellent good, i'faith.
SIR TOBY. Good, good.
CLOWN.

> *What is love? 'tis not hereafter;*
> *Present mirth hath present laughter;*
>   *What's to come is still unsure.*
> *In delay there lies no plenty;*
> *Then come kiss me, sweet and twenty;[101]*
>   *Youth's a stuff will not endure.*

SIR ANDREW. A mellifluous voice, as I am true knight.
SIR TOBY. A contagious breath.
SIR ANDREW. Very sweet and contagious, i'faith.
SIR TOBY. To hear by the nose, it is dulcet in contagion. But shall we
    make the welkin dance indeed?[102] Shall we rouse the night-owl in a
    catch that will draw three souls out of one weaver?[103] shall we do
    that?
SIR ANDREW. An you love me, let's do't: I am dog at a catch.
CLOWN. By'r lady, sir, and some dogs will catch well.

---

[99] That is, a civil and virtuous song; so described in *The Mad Pranks of Robin Goodfellow.*

[100] "This song probably was not written by Shakespeare. Chappell, in his *Popular Music of the Olden Time*, says the tune is in Queen Elizabeth's Virginal Book, arranged by Byrd. He also says it was printed in 1599; and from this he concludes "either that Shakespeare's *Twelfth Night* was written in or before that year, or that in accordance with the then prevailing custom, *O mistress mine* was an old song, introduced into the play." Dyce thinks "the latter supposition is doubtless the true one."

[101] *Sweet-and-twenty* appears to have been an old term of endearment.

[102] Drink till the sky seems to turn round.

[103] Shakespeare represents weavers as much given to harmony in his time. Sir Toby meant that the catch should be so harmonious that it would hale the soul out of a weaver *thrice over.*

SIR ANDREW. Most certain: let our catch be, *Thou knave.*

CLOWN. *Hold thy peace, thou knave*, knight? I shall be constrain'd in't to call thee knave, knight.

SIR ANDREW. 'Tis not the first time I have constrained one to call me knave. Begin, fool; it begins, *Hold thy peace.*

CLOWN. I shall never begin if I hold my peace.

SIR ANDREW. Good, i'faith! Come, begin.

[*They sing a catch.*]

[*Enter* MARIA.]

MARIA. What a caterwauling do you keep here! If my lady have not called up her steward Malvolio, and bid him turn you out of doors, never trust me.

SIR TOBY. My lady's a Cataian,[104] we are politicians; Malvolio's a Peg-a-Ramsey, and *Three merry men be we.* Am not I consanguineous? am I not of her blood? Tilly-valley, lady![105]— [*Sings.*] *There dwelt a man in Babylon, lady, lady!*

CLOWN. Beshrew me, the knight's in admirable fooling.

SIR ANDREW. Ay, he does well enough if he be disposed, and so do I too; he does it with a better grace, but I do it more natural.

SIR TOBY. [*Sings.*] *O'*[106] *the twelfth day of December,*[107]—

MARIA. For the love o' God, peace!

[*Enter* MALVOLIO.]

MALVOLIO. My masters, are you mad? or what are you? Have you no wit, manners, nor honesty, but to gabble like tinkers at this time of night? Do ye make an ale-house of my lady's house, that ye squeak out your coziers'[108] catches without any mitigation or remorse of voice? Is there no respect of place, persons, nor time, in you?

---

[104] This word generally signified a sharper. Sir Toby is too drunk for precision, and uses it merely as a term of reproach.

[105] An interjection of contempt, equivalent to *fiddle-fiddle*.

[106] This is not the interjectional *O*, but the elided preposition *on* or *of*;

[107] With Sir Toby as wine goes in music comes out, and fresh songs keep bubbling up in his memory as he waxes mellower. A similar thing occurs in *Henry IV., Part 2* where Master Silence grows merry and musical amidst his cups in "the sweet of the night." Of the ballads referred to by Sir Toby, *O' the twelfth day of December* is entirely lost. Percy has one stanza of *There dwelt a man in Babylon*, which he describes as "a poor dull performance, and very long." *Three merry men be we* seems to have been the burden of several old songs, one of which was called *Robin Hood and the Tanner*. *Peg-a-Ramsey*, or *Peggy Ramsey*, was an old popular tune which had several ballads fitted to it. *Thou knave* was a catch which, says Sir John Hawkins, "appears to be so contrived that each of the singers calls the other knave in turn."

[108] *Coziers* is *botchers*, whether botching with the needles or with awls.

SIR TOBY. We did keep time, sir, in our catches. Snick-up![109]

MALVOLIO. Sir Toby, I must be round[110] with you. My lady bade me tell you that, though she harbours you as her kinsman she's nothing allied to your disorders. If you can separate yourself and your misdemeanours, you are welcome to the house; if not, an it would please you to take leave of her, she is very willing to bid you farewell.

SIR TOBY. [*Sings.*] *Farewell, dear heart, since I must needs be gone.*[111]

MARIA. Nay, good Sir Toby.

CLOWN. [*Sings.*] *His eyes do show his days are almost done.*

MALVOLIO. Is't even so?

SIR TOBY. *But I will never die.*

CLOWN. Sir Toby, there you lie.

MALVOLIO. This is much credit to you.

SIR TOBY. [*Sings.*] *Shall I bid him go?*

CLOWN. [*Sings.*] *What an if you do?*

SIR TOBY. [*Sings.*] *Shall I bid him go, and spare not?*

CLOWN. [*Sings.*] *O, no, no, no, no, you dare not.*

SIR TOBY. Out o' tune? sir, ye lie. Art any more than a steward? Dost thou think, because thou art virtuous, there shall be no more cakes and ale?

CLOWN. Yes, by Saint Anne; and ginger shall be hot i' the mouth too.

SIR TOBY. Thou'art i' the right.—Go, sir, rub your chain with crumbs.[112]—A stoup of wine, Maria!

MALVOLIO. Mistress Mary, if you prized my lady's favour at anything more than contempt, you would not give means for this uncivil rule; she shall know of it, by this hand. [*Exit.*]

MARIA. Go shake your ears.[113]

SIR ANDREW. 'Twere as good a deed as to drink when a man's a-hungry, to challenge him the field, and then to break promise with him and make a fool of him.

---

[109] *Snick-up* was an exclamation of contempt, equivalent to "Go hang yourself," or "go and be hanged."

[110] *Round* is *downright* or *plain-spoken.*

[111] This is the first line of an old ballad, entitled *Corydon's Farewell to Phillis.* It was inserted in Percy's *Reliques* from an ancient miscellany, called *The Golden Garland of Princely Delights.* The musical dialogue that follows between Sir Toby and the Clown is adapted to their purpose from the first two stanzas of the ballad.

[112] Stewards anciently wore a chain of silver or gold, as a mark of superiority, as did other principal servants. Wolsey's chief cook is described by Cavendish as wearing "velvet or satin with a chain of gold." One of the methods used to clean gilt plate was *rubbing it with crumbs.* So in Webster's *Duchess of Malfi*: "Yea, and the chippings of the buttery fly after him, to *scour his gold chain.*"

[113] "Shake your ears" is probably used as a metaphor implying that Malvolio has *long ears*; in other words, that he is an *ass.*

SIR TOBY. Do't, knight; I'll write thee a challenge; or I'll deliver thy indignation to him by word of mouth.

MARIA. Sweet Sir Toby, be patient for to-night; since the youth of the count's was to-day with my lady, she is much out of quiet. For Monsieur Malvolio, let me alone with him: if I do not gull him into a nayword,[114] and make him a common recreation, do not think I have wit enough to lie straight in my bed. I know I can do it.

SIR TOBY. Possess us,[115] possess us; tell us something of him.

MARIA. Marry, sir, sometimes he is a kind of Puritan.

SIR ANDREW. O, if I thought that, I'd beat him like a dog!

SIR TOBY. What, for being a Puritan? thy exquisite reason, dear knight?

SIR ANDREW. I have no exquisite reason for't, but I have reason good enough.

MARIA. The Devil a Puritan that he is, or anything constantly but a time-pleaser: an affection'd ass,[116] that cons state without book and utters it by great swaths:[117] the best persuaded of himself, so crammed, as he thinks, with excellences, that it is his grounds of faith that all that look on him love him; and on that vice in him will my revenge find notable cause to work.

SIR TOBY. What wilt thou do?

MARIA. I will drop in his way some obscure epistles of love; wherein, by the colour of his beard, the shape of his leg, the manner of his gait, the expressure of his eye, forehead, and complexion, he shall find himself most feelingly personated. I can write very like my lady, your niece; on a forgotten matter we can hardly make distinction of our hands.

SIR TOBY. Excellent! I smell a device.

SIR ANDREW. I have't in my nose too.

SIR TOBY. He shall think, by the letters that thou wilt drop, that they come from my niece, and that she is in love with him.

MARIA. My purpose is, indeed, a horse of that colour.

SIR ANDREW. And your horse now would make him an ass.

MARIA. Ass, I doubt not.

SIR ANDREW. O 'twill be admirable!

MARIA. Sport royal, I warrant you. I know my physic will work with him. I will plant you two, and let the Fool make a third, where he

---

[114] *Nay-word* here means *by-word* or *laughing-stock*. So defined in an old dictionary. Elsewhere the Poet has it in the sense of *watch-word.*

[115] *Possess* for *inform*; a very frequent usage.

[116] An *affected ass. Affection* was often used for *affectation.*

[117] By great parcels or heaps. *Swaths* are the rows of grass left by the scythe of the mower. Maria means that he is full of political strut, and spouts arguments of State by rote.

shall find the letter; observe his construction of it. For this night, to bed, and dream on the event. Farewell. [*Exit.*]

SIR TOBY. Good night, Penthesilea.[118]

SIR ANDREW. Before me, she's a good wench.

SIR TOBY. She's a beagle,[119] true bred, and one that adores me. What o' that?

SIR ANDREW. I was adored once too.

SIR TOBY. Let's to bed, knight. Thou hadst need send for more money.

SIR ANDREW. If I cannot recover your niece I am a foul way out.

SIR TOBY. Send for money, knight; if thou hast her not i' the end, call me cut.[120]

SIR ANDREW. If I do not, never trust me; take it how you will.

SIR TOBY. Come, come; I'll go burn some sack;[121] 'tis too late to go to bed now: come, knight; come, knight. [*Exeunt.*]

SCENE IV.

An Apartment in the DUKE'*s Palace.*

[*Enter* DUKE, VIOLA, CURIO, *and others.*]

DUKE. Give me some music:—now, good morrow, friends:—
    Now, good Cesario, but that piece of song,
    That old and antique song we heard last night:
    Methought it did relieve my passion much;
    More than light airs and recollected terms[122]
    Of these most brisk and giddy-paced times.
    Come, but one verse.

CURIO. He is not here, so please your lordship, that should sing it.

DUKE. Who was it?

---

[118] Penthesilea was Queen of the Amazons, and killed by Achilles in the Trojan War; *politely.*

[119] A *beagle* was a small hound, and a keen hunter; applied to Maria from her brevity of person and sharpness of wit.

[120] *Cut* was a common contraction of *curtail.* One of the carriers' horses in *Henry IV.* is called *Cut.*

[121] *Sack* is an old term for *sherry wine,* which appears to have been Sir Toby's favourite beverage, as it was also Falstaff's. The phrase "*burnt* sack" occurs twice in *The Merry Wives*; perhaps a preparation of sack and other ingredients finished for the mouth, as flip used to be, by thrusting a red-hot iron into it.

[122] This is commonly explained as meaning *repeated* terms, or the repetition of poetical and musical phrases. Some think terms refers to a sort of lyrical embroidery made by running culled expressions together, and so lacking the plainness and simplicity that goes to the heart. *Old and antique,* two lines before, is not a pleonasm, *antique* carrying a sense of quaintness as well as of age.

CURIO. Feste, the jester, my lord; a fool that the Lady Olivia's father
    took much delight in: he is about the house.
DUKE. Go seek him out:—and play the tune the while.—

    [*Exit* CURIO. *Music.*]

    Come hither, boy. If ever thou shalt love,
    In the sweet pangs of it remember me;
    For, such as I am, all true lovers are,—
    Unstaid and skittish in all motions else,
    Save in the constant image of the creature
    That is belov'd.—How dost thou like this tune?
VIOLA. It gives a very echo to the seat
    Where Love is throned.
DUKE. Thou dost speak masterly:
    My life upon't, young though thou art, thine eye
    Hath stayed upon some favour[123] that it loves;
    Hath it not, boy?
VIOLA. A little, by your favour.
DUKE. What kind of woman is't?
VIOLA. Of your complexion.
DUKE. She is not worth thee, then. What years, i'faith?
VIOLA. About your years, my lord.
DUKE. Too old, by Heaven! Let still the woman take
    An elder than herself; so wears she to him,
    So sways she level in her husband's heart.
    For, boy, however we do praise ourselves,
    Our fancies are more giddy and unfirm,
    More longing, wavering, sooner lost and won,
    Than women's are.
VIOLA. I think it well, my lord.
DUKE. Then let thy love be younger than thyself,
    Or thy affection cannot hold the bent:
    For women are as roses, whose fair flower,
    Being once display'd, doth fall that very hour.
VIOLA. And so they are: alas, that they are so,—
    To die, even when they to perfection grow!

    [*Re-enter* CURIO *and* CLOWN.]

DUKE. O, fellow, come, the song we had last night.—
    Mark it, Cesario; it is old and plain:
    The spinsters and the knitters in the sun,

---

[123] *Favour* for *feature.* Viola in her reply plays upon the word.

And the free[124] maids, that weave their thread with bones,
Do use to chant it: it is silly sooth,[125]
And dallies with the innocence of love
Like the old age.[126]
CLOWN. Are you ready, sir?
DUKE. Ay; pr'ythee, sing. [*Music.*]
CLOWN.

SONG.

Come away, come away, death.
    And in sad cypress[127] let me be laid;
Fly away, fly away, breath;
    I am slain by a fair cruel maid.
My shroud of white, stuck all with yew,
    O, prepare it!
My part of death no one so true
    Did share it.[128]

Not a flower, not a flower sweet,
    On my black coffin let there be strown:
Not a friend, not a friend greet
    My poor corpse where my bones shall be thrown:
A thousand thousand sighs to save,
    Lay me, O, where
Sad true lover never find my grave,
    To weep there!

DUKE. There's for thy pains.
CLOWN. No pains, sir; I take pleasure in singing, sir.
DUKE. I'll pay thy pleasure, then.
CLOWN. Truly, sir, and pleasure will be paid one time or another.
DUKE. Give me now leave to leave thee.[129]

---

[124] *Free* appears to have been often used in the sense of *pure* or *chaste*. So, in *The Winter's Tale*, ii. 3, Hermione is described as "a gracious innocent soul, more *free* than he is jealous." It may, however, mean *frank, unsuspecting*; the proper style of a plain and guileless heart.

[125] *Silly sooth* is *simple truth.*

[126] The *old age* is the *ages past*, times of simplicity.

[127] Cypress wood was thought to be the fittest for coffins.—*Come away* here means *come on*, or *come*, simply. Repeatedly so.

[128] Death is a part in the drama of life, which all have to undergo or to act; and the thought here seems to be, that, "of all the actors who have shared in this common lot, I am the truest," or, "no one has been so true as I."

[129] Probably the Duke's polite way of requesting the Clown to leave. Some, however, think the text corrupt; and so indeed it may be.

CLOWN. Now the melancholy god protect thee; and the tailor make thy doublet of changeable taffeta, for thy mind is a very opal!¹³⁰ I would have men of such constancy put to sea, that their business might be everything, and their intent everywhere; for that's it that always makes a good voyage of nothing. Farewell. [*Exit.*]

DUKE. Let all the rest give place.—

[*Exeunt* CURIO *and* ATTENDANTS.]

    Once more, Cesario,
Get thee to yond same sovereign cruelty:
Tell her my love, more noble than the world,
Prizes not quantity of dirty lands;
The parts that Fortune hath bestow'd upon her,
Tell her, I hold as giddily as Fortune;
But 'tis that miracle and queen of gems
That Nature pranks her in attracts my soul.

VIOLA. But if she cannot love you, sir?

DUKE. I cannot be so answer'd.

VIOLA. 'Sooth, but you must.
Say that some lady—as, perhaps, there is—
Hath for your love as great a pang of heart
As you have for Olivia: you cannot love her;
You tell her so. Must she not then be answer'd?

DUKE. There is no woman's sides
Can bide the beating of so strong a passion
As love doth give my heart: no woman's heart
So big to hold so much; they lack retention.¹³¹
Alas, their love may be called appetite,—
No motion of the liver,¹³² but the palate,—
That suffer surfeit, cloyment, and revolt;
But mine is all as hungry as the sea,
And can digest as much: make no compare
Between that love a woman can bear me
And that I owe Olivia.

VIOLA. Ay, but I know,—

DUKE. What dost thou know?

VIOLA. Too well what love women to men may owe.

---

¹³⁰ The opal is a gem that varies its hues, as it is viewed in different lights, like what is sometimes called *changeable silk,* that is, *taffeta.* "The melancholy god" is Saturn; hence the word *saturnine,* which means *sad* or *gloomy.*

¹³¹ *Retention* here evidently has the sense of *capacity.* A rather singular use of the word; but the Poet has it so again in his 122d Sonnet: "That poor *retention* could not hold so much."—"So big, to hold" is "so big, *as* to hold"; an ellipsis occurring very often.

¹³² The *liver* was thought to be the special seat of love and courage.

In faith, they are as true of heart as we.
My father had a daughter loved a man,
As it might be perhaps, were I a woman,
I should your lordship.
DUKE. And what's her history?
VIOLA. A blank, my lord. She never told her love,
But let concealment, like a worm i' the bud,
Feed on her damask cheek: she pined in thought;[133]
And with a green and yellow melancholy,
She sat like patience on a monument,
Smiling at grief.[134] Was not this love, indeed?
We men may say more, swear more; but indeed,
Our shows are more than will; for still we prove
Much in our vows, but little in our love.
DUKE. But died thy sister of her love, my boy?
VIOLA. I am all the daughters of my father's house,
And all the brothers too;—and yet I know not.—
Sir, shall I to this lady?
DUKE. Ay, that's the theme.
To her in haste: give her this jewel; say
My love can give no place, bide no denay.[135] [*Exeunt.*]

SCENE V.

OLIVIA's *garden.*

[*Enter* SIR TOBY BELCH, SIR ANDREW AGUECHEEK, *and* FABIAN.]

SIR TOBY. Come thy ways, Signior Fabian.
FABIAN. Nay, I'll come; if I lose a scruple of this sport let me be boiled to death with melancholy.[136]

---

[133] The meaning is, "she wasted away through grief." So in Hamlet's soliloquy: "The native hue of resolution is sicklied o'er with the pale cast of thought"; that is, the pale complexion of grief. And in *Julius Cæsar*, ii. 1: "If he love Cæsar, all that he can do is to himself; take thought and die for Caesar"; where *take thought and die* means "grieve himself to death." So, again, in St. Matthew, vi. 25: "Take no thought for your life, what ye shall eat, or what ye shall drink;" &c.

[134] She sat smiling at grief as the image of Patience sits on a monument.

[135] *Denay* is an old form of *denial*; used here for the rhyme.

[136] *Melancholy* must be used here to signify a form of *madness* or *lunacy*; something such as Milton has in view, in *Paradise Lost*, x. i. 485: "Demoniac frenzy, moping *melancholy*, and moon-struck madness." Shakespeare repeatedly supposes the brains of crazy people to be in a bailing or highly feverish state; as in *A Midsummer*, v. 1: "Lovers and madmen have such *seething* brains."

SIR TOBY. Wouldst thou not be glad to have the niggardly rascally sheep-biter[137] come by some notable shame?

FABIAN. I would exult, man; you know he brought me out o' favour with my lady about a bear-baiting here.

SIR TOBY. To anger him we'll have the bear again; and we will fool him black and blue:[138]—shall we not, Sir Andrew?

SIR ANDREW. An we do not, it is pity of our lives.

SIR TOBY. Here comes the little villain:—

[*Enter* MARIA.]

How now, my metal of India![139]

MARIA. Get ye all three into the box-tree: Malvolio's coming down this walk; he has been yonder i' the sun practising behaviour to his own shadow this half hour: observe him, for the love of mockery; for I know this letter will make a contemplative idiot of him. Close, in the name of jesting! [*The men hide themselves.*]—Lie thou there; [*Throws down a letter.*] for here comes the trout that must be caught with tickling. [*Exit.*]

[*Enter* MALVOLIO.]

MALVOLIO. 'Tis but fortune; all is fortune. Maria once told me she did affect me: and I have heard herself come thus near, that, should she fancy, it should be one of my complexion. Besides, she uses me with a more exalted respect than any one else that follows her. What should I think on't?

SIR TOBY. Here's an overweening rogue!

---

[137] *Sheep-biter*, says Dyce, was "a cant term for a *thief.*" But I do not well see how it should be applied to Malvolio in that sense. In *Measure for Measure*, v. 1, Lucio says to the Duke, who is disguised as a Friar, "Show your knave's visage, with a pox to you! show your sheep-biting face." Here *sheep-biting*, as also *sheep-biter* in the text, seems to have the sense of *morose, censorious, fault-finding*, or given to biting unoffending persons with harsh language. In Chapman's *May-Day*, iii. 1, a lecherous, intriguing old rogue, named Lorenzo, has a sharp trick played upon him by his nephew Lodovico, who speaks of him as follows: "Alas, poor uncle, I have monstrously abused him; and yet marvellous worthy, for he disparageth the whole blood of us; and I wish all such old *sheep-biters* might dip their fingers in such sauce to their mutton."

[138] I can hardly imagine what this means, having never met with the phrase anywhere else, that I remember. What it is to be flogged *black and blue* I have ample cause to know: but to be *fooled* black and blue, what is it? Is it to mock one, till he turns black in the face from anger and vexation? The best I can do with it is by quoting from one of Mr. Mantalini's speeches in *Nicholas Nickleby*: "What a demnition long time have you kept me ringing at this confounded old cracked tea-kettle of a bell, every tinkle of which is enough to throw a strong man into *blue convulsions*, upon my life and soul, oh demmit."

[139] "Metal of India" probably means *precious girl*, or *heart of gold*.

FABIAN. O, peace! Contemplation makes a rare turkey-cock of him; how he jets under his advanced plumes![140]

SIR ANDREW. 'Slight,[141] I could so beat the rogue!

SIR TOBY. Peace, I say.

MALVOLIO. To be Count Malvolio:—

SIR TOBY. Ah, rogue!

SIR ANDREW. Pistol him, pistol him.

SIR TOBY. Peace, peace.

MALVOLIO.—there is example for't; the lady of the strachy[142] married the yeoman of the wardrobe.

SIR ANDREW. Fie on him, Jezebel!

FABIAN. O, peace! now he's deeply in; look how imagination blows him.[143]

MALVOLIO. Having been three months married to her, sitting in my state,—

SIR TOBY. O for a stone-bow,[144] to hit him in the eye!

MALVOLIO.—calling my officers about me, in my branched velvet gown; having come from a day-bed, where I have left Olivia sleeping;—

SIR TOBY. Fire and brimstone!

FABIAN. O, peace, peace.

MALVOLIO.—and then to have the humour of state: and after a demure travel of regard,[145]—telling them I know my place as I would they should do theirs,—to ask for my kinsman Toby.—

SIR TOBY. Bolts and shackles!

FABIAN. O, peace, peace, peace! now, now.

MALVOLIO.—Seven of my people, with an obedient start, make out for him: I frown the while, and perchance, wind up my watch, or

---

[140] To *jet* is to *strut* with pride. So in *Cymbeline*, iii. 3: "The gates of monarchs are arch'd so high, that giants may *jet* through, and keep their impious turbans on, without good morrow to the Sun."—*Advanced plumes* is *raised* or *uplifted feathers*.

[141] *'Slight!* is a disguised oath, for *God's light!*

[142] Payne Knight conjectured that *strachy* was a corruption of the Italian *stratico*, a word derived from the low Latin *strategus*, or *straticus*, and often used for the governor of a city or province. But Mr. A. E. Brae offers, I think, a more probable explanation: "Florio, in his *Italian Dictionary*, has a word very like in sound to this *strachy*: 'Stratisco, the train or long garment of state worn by a princess.' And when it is considered that there is a sort of appositeness in making the lady who wears the train condescend to marry the man who had charge of it, it offers, I think, a very probable interpretation of Malvolio's meaning." He also quotes from Camden's *Remains* an epitaph showing that "yeoman of the wardrobe" was a well known office in the households of high-born ladies: "Her lyes Richard Hobbs, Yeoman of the roabes to our late sovereigne Queene Mary."

[143] *Puffs him up*. So in Bacon's *Advancement of Learning*: "Knowledge *bloweth* up, but charity buildeth up."

[144] A bow for hurling stones.

[145] This seems to be a Malvolian phrase for a stern and awful gaze or stare, with an air of dignified contempt.

play with some rich jewel. Toby approaches; curtsies[146] there to me:—

SIR TOBY. Shall this fellow live?

FABIAN. Though our silence be drawn from us with cars, yet peace.

MALVOLIO.—I extend my hand to him thus, quenching my familiar smile with an austere regard of control,[147]—

SIR TOBY. And does not Toby take you a blow o' the lips then?

MALVOLIO.—saying, *Cousin Toby, my fortunes having cast me on your niece, give me this prerogative of speech;*—

SIR TOBY. What, what?

MALVOLIO.—*you must amend your drunkenness.*—

SIR TOBY. Out, scab?

FABIAN. Nay, patience, or we break the sinews of our plot.

MALVOLIO.—*Besides, you waste the treasure of your time with a foolish knight,*—

SIR ANDREW. That's me, I warrant you.

MALVOLIO.—*one Sir Andrew.*

SIR ANDREW. I knew 'twas I; for many do call me fool.

MALVOLIO. What employment have we here?

[*Taking up the letter.*]

FABIAN. Now is the woodcock near the gin.[148]

SIR TOBY. O, peace! And the spirit of humours intimate reading aloud to him![149]

MALVOLIO. By my life, this is my lady's hand: these be her very *C's*, her *U's*, and her *T's*; and thus makes she her great P's. It is in contempt of question, her hand.

SIR ANDREW. Her *C's*, her *U's*, and her *T's*. Why that?

MALVOLIO. [*Reads.*] *To the unknown beloved, this, and my good wishes*: Her very phrases!—[Opening the letter.] By your leave, wax.—Soft!—and the impressure her Lucrece, with which she uses to seal: 'tis my lady. To whom should this be?

FABIAN. This wins him, liver and all.

---

[146] *Curtsy* was used, to denote acts of civility and reverence by either sex.

[147] "An austere regard of control" probably means such a look of sternness as would awe down or repress any approaches of familiarity.

[148] The woodcock was thought to be the stupidest of birds; and *gin* was but another word for *trap* or *snare*.

[149] "May the self-love-sick humour that possesses him prompt him to read the letter aloud! "Sir Toby wants to hear the contents, and also to see Malvolio smack his lips over the "dish of poison."

MALVOLIO. [*Reads.*]

> *Jove knows I love:*
> *But who?*
> *Lips, do not move;*
> *No man must know.*

No man must know. What follows? the numbers alter'd![150]
No man must know. If this should be thee, Malvolio?
SIR TOBY. Marry, hang thee, brock![151]
MALVOLIO. [*Reads.*]

> *I may command where I adore:*
> *But silence, like a Lucrece knife,*
> *With bloodless stroke my heart doth gore;*
> *M, O, A, I, doth sway my life.*

FABIAN. A fustian riddle!
SIR TOBY. Excellent wench, say I.
MALVOLIO. *M, O, A, I, doth sway my life.*—Nay, but first let me see,
  let me see, let me see.
FABIAN. What dish of poison has she dressed him![152]
SIR TOBY. And with what wing the staniel checks at it![153]
MALVOLIO. *I may command where I adore.* Why, she may command
  me: I serve her, she is my lady. Why, this is evident to any formal
  capacity;[154] there is no obstruction in this;—And the end,—What
  should that alphabetical position portend? If I could make that
  resemble something in me.—Softly!—*M, O, A, I.*—
SIR TOBY. O, ay, make up that:—he is now at a cold scent.[155]
FABIAN. Sowter will cry upon't for all this, though it be as rank as a
  fox.[156]

---

[150] Referring, no doubt, to the *different versification* of what follows. The use of *numbers* for *verse* is quite common; as in Milton's "harmonious *numbers*," and Pope's "I lisped in *numbers*, for the numbers came."

[151] *Brock* is *badger*, and was used as a term of contempt.

[152] An exclamative speech. We should say "What a dish," &c.

[153] The *staniel* is a species of hawk, which inhabits old buildings and rocks. To check, says Latham in his *Book of Falconry*, is, "when crows, rocks, pies, or other birds coming in view of the hawk, she forsaketh her natural flight to fly at them."

[154] To any one *in his senses*, or whose *capacity* is not out of *form*.

[155] A *cold scent* is a trail that has grown so faint as not to be traceable by the smell, or hardly so.

[156] *Sowter* is used here as the name of a hound.—The Poet sometimes has *though* in a causal, not a concessive, sense; that is, as equivalent to *because, for, since*, or *inasmuch as*. In such cases, his meaning naturally appears to us just the opposite of what it really is. So, here, *though it be* stands for *since* or *because it is*. The logic of the passage requires it to be so understood; for, when a bound loses the trail, he snuffs all round till he recovers

MALVOLIO. *M,*—Malvolio; *M,*—why, that begins my name.
FABIAN. Did not I say he would work it out?
    The cur is excellent at faults.[157]
MALVOLIO. *M,*—But then there is no consonancy in the sequel; that
    suffers under probation:[158] *A* should follow, but *O* does.
FABIAN. And *O* shall end, I hope.
SIR TOBY. Ay, or I'll cudgel him, and make him cry *O!*
MALVOLIO. And then *I* comes behind.
FABIAN. Ay, an you had any eye behind you, you might see more
    detraction at your heels than fortunes before you.
MALVOLIO. *M, O, A, I*; this simulation[159] is not as the former: and
    yet, to crush this a little, it would bow to me, for every one of these
    letters are in my name. Soft; here follows prose.

—[*Reads.*] If this fall into thy hand, revolve. In my stars I am
above thee; but be not afraid of greatness. Some are born great,
some achieve greatness, and some have greatness thrust upon
them. Thy fates open their hands; let thy blood and spirit embrace
them. And, to inure thyself to what thou art like to be, cast thy
humble slough and appear fresh. Be opposite with a kinsman, surly
with servants: let thy tongue tang arguments of state; put thyself
into the trick of singularity: She thus advises thee that sighs for
thee. Remember who commended thy yellow stockings, and
wished to see thee ever cross-garter'd.[160] I say, remember. Go to;
thou art made, if thou desirest to be so; if not, let me see thee a
steward still, the fellow of servants, and not worthy to touch
fortune's fingers. Farewell. She that would alter services with thee,
'The fortunate-unhappy.'

Daylight and champaign discovers not more:[161] this is open. I will
be proud, I will read politic authors, I will baffle Sir Toby, I will

---

it, and then sets up a peculiar howl, "cries upon't," and starts off afresh in the pursuit.
"Giving mouth" is the technical phrase for it; and Mr. Joseph Crosby writes me that "it is
a cry well known both to the sportsmen and also to the rest of the pack, which
immediately opens in concert."

    [157] A *fault*, in the language of the chase, is a breach in the continuity of the trail, so
that the hound loses the scent, and has to trace or snuff it out anew.

    [158] That is, *fails* or *breaks down* on being *tried* or *put to the proof.*

    [159] *Simulation* for *resemblance* or *similarity.* Malvolio cannot so easily find himself
pointed out here as in what has gone before.

    [160] A fashion once prevailed for some time of wearing the garters *crossed* on the
leg. Rich and expensive garters worn below the knee were then in use. Olivia's
detestation of these fashions probably arose from thinking them coxcombical.

    [161] *Champain* is open-level country, affording a free prospect.

wash off gross acquaintance, I will be point-device,[162] the very man. I do not now fool myself to let imagination jade me; for every reason excites to this, that my lady loves me. She did commend my yellow stockings of late, she did praise my leg being cross-gartered; and in this she manifests herself to my love, and with a kind of injunction, drives me to these habits of her liking. I thank my stars I am happy. I will be strange, stout,[163] in yellow stockings, and cross-gartered, even with the swiftness of putting on. Jove and my stars be praised!—Here is yet a postscript.

[*Reads.*] Thou canst not choose but know who I am. If thou entertainest my love, let it appear in thy smiling; thy smiles become thee well: therefore in my presence still smile, dear my sweet, I pr'ythee.' Jove, I thank thee. I will smile; I will do everything that thou wilt have me. [*Exit.*]

FABIAN. I will not give my part of this sport for a pension of thousands to be paid from the Sophy.[164]

SIR TOBY. I could marry this wench for this device,—

SIR ANDREW. So could I too.

SIR TOBY. And ask no other dowry with her but such another jest.

SIR ANDREW. Nor I neither.

FABIAN. Here comes my noble gull-catcher.

[*Re-enter* MARIA.]

SIR TOBY. Wilt thou set thy foot o' my neck?

SIR ANDREW. [*to* MARIA.] Or o' mine either?

SIR TOBY. [*to* MARIA.] Shall I play my freedom at tray-trip,[165] and become thy bond-slave?

SIR ANDREW. [*to* MARIA.] I' faith, or I either?

SIR TOBY. [*to* MARIA.] Why, thou hast put him in such a dream, that, when the image of it leaves him, he must run mad.

MARIA. Nay, but say true; does it work upon him?

SIR TOBY. Like aqua-vitae with a midwife.

---

[162] "I will be punctiliously exacting and precise in all the dues and becomings of my rank."—To baffle, as the word is here used, is to *triumph over*, to *treat contemptuously*, or to *put down*.

[163] *Strange*, here, is *reserved, distant*, or *standing aloof*, and on his dignity. And *stout* is in "a concatenation accordingly"; that is, *haughty, overbearing*, or *stout-tempered*.

[164] *Sophy* was the Persian title of majesty. At the time this play was written, Sir Robert Shirley had lately returned as ambassador from the Sophy. Sir Robert boasted of the great rewards he had received, and cut a big dash in London.

[165] *Tray-trip* was probably a game of dice; though some hold it to have been the game of draughts. So in an old satire called *Machiavel's Dog*: "But, leaving cards, let's go to *dice* awhile; to passage, *treitrippe*, hazard, or mum-chance."—*Play my freedom* means play *for* my freedom; that is, *stake it*.

MARIA. If you will then see the fruits of the sport, mark his first approach before my lady: he will come to her in yellow stockings, and 'tis a colour she abhors, and cross-gartered, a fashion she detests; and he will smile upon her, which will now be so unsuitable to her disposition, being addicted to a melancholy as she is, that it cannot but turn him into a notable contempt; if you will see it, follow me.

SIR TOBY. To the gates of Tartar,[166] thou most excellent Devil of wit!

SIR ANDREW. I'll make one too. [*Exeunt.*]

ACT III.

SCENE I.

OLIVIA'*s Garden.*

[*Enter* VIOLA, *and the* CLOWN *with a tabor.*]

VIOLA. Save thee, friend, and thy music! dost thou live by thy tabor?[167]

CLOWN. No, sir, I live by the church.

VIOLA. Art thou a churchman?[168]

CLOWN. No such matter, sir: I do live by the church; for I do live at my house, and my house doth stand by the church.

VIOLA. So thou mayst say the king lies by a beggar, if a beggar dwell near him; or the church stands by thy tabor, if thy tabor stand by the church.

CLOWN. You have said,[169] sir. To see this age!—A sentence is but a cheveril glove to a good wit:[170] How quickly the wrong side may be turned outward!

VIOLA. Nay, that's certain; they that dally nicely with words may quickly make them wanton.

CLOWN. I would, therefore, my sister had had no name, sir.

VIOLA. Why, man?

CLOWN. Why, sir, her name's a word; and to dally with that word might make my sister wanton. But indeed words are very rascals, since bonds disgraced them.[171]

---

[166] *Tartar* is the old Tartarus or Hades. Note the sympathy of *Tartar* and *devil.*

[167] It seems that the "allowed Fool" had a prescriptive right to the *tabor* as his musical instrument. Tarleton, the famous stage jester, is represented as armed with one, in a cut prefixed to his *Jests*, 1611.

[168] *Churchman* was in common use for *clergyman.*

[169] This form of assent or affirmation, now obsolete, occurs in the Bible; as in our Lord's answer to Pilate, St. Mark, xv. 2: "Thou sayest it."

[170] A *cheveril* glove is a *kid* glove. The term was used much as *India rubber* is now. So in one of Ray's proverbs: "He hath a conscience like a *cheveril's* skin."

VIOLA. Thy reason, man?

CLOWN. Troth, sir, I can yield you none without words; and words are grown so false I am loath to prove reason with them.

VIOLA. I warrant, thou art a merry fellow, and carest for nothing.

CLOWN. Not so, sir, I do care for something: but in my conscience, sir, I do not care for you; if that be to care for nothing, sir, I would it would make you invisible.

VIOLA. Art not thou the Lady Olivia's fool?

CLOWN. No, indeed, sir; the Lady Olivia has no folly: she will keep no fool, sir, till she be married; and fools are as like husbands as pilchards are to herrings,[172]—the husband's the bigger; I am, indeed, not her fool, but her corrupter of words.

VIOLA. I saw thee late at the Count Orsino's.

CLOWN. Foolery, sir, does walk about the orb like the sun; it shines everywhere. I would be sorry, sir, but[173] the fool should be as oft with your master as with my mistress: I think I saw your wisdom there.

VIOLA. Nay, an thou pass[174] upon me, I'll no more with thee.
Hold, there's expenses for thee. [*Gives a piece of money.*]

CLOWN. Now Jove, in his next commodity of hair, send thee a beard!

VIOLA. By my troth, I'll tell thee, I am almost sick for one; though I would not have it grow on my chin. Is thy lady within?

CLOWN. Would not a pair of these breed,[175] sir?

VIOLA. Yes, being kept together and put to use.

CLOWN. I would play Lord Pandarus of Phrygia, sir, to bring a Cressida to this Troilus.

VIOLA. I understand you, sir; 'tis well begged. [*Gives another piece of money.*]

CLOWN. The matter, I hope, is not great, sir, begging but a beggar: Cressida was a beggar.[176] My lady is within, sir. I will construe to

---

[171] This probably alludes to an order of the Privy Council, in June, 1600, laying very severe restrictions on the Poet's art. The order, besides that it allowed only two houses to be used for stage-plays in the city and suburbs, interdicted those two from playing at all during Lent, or in any time of great sickness, and also limited them to twice a week at all other times. If rigidly enforced it would have amounted almost to a total suppression of playhouses. As the penalty was imprisonment, it might well be said that words were disgraced by bonds.

[172] Pilchards are said to differ from herrings only in that they can be fried in their own fat, whereas herrings have not fat enough for that purpose.

[173] *But* is here equivalent to *if not.*

[174] *Pass* for *make a pass, thrust,* or *sally,* of *wit.*

[175] The Fool is quirkishly asking for a *mate* to the piece of money Viola has given him.

[176] This famous jilt-heroine is thus addressed in Henryson's *Testament of Cresseid*: "Great penurye shalt thou suffer, and as a *beggar* dye." And again:

Thou shalt go begging from hous to hous,

them whence you come; who you are and what you would are out
of my welkin,—I might say element,[177] but the word is overworn.
[*Exit.*]

VIOLA. This fellow's wise enough to play the Fool;
    And, to do that well, craves a kind of wit:
    He must observe their mood on whom he jests,
    The quality of persons, and the time;
    And, like the haggard, check at every feather
    That comes before his eye.[178] This is a practice
    As full of labour as a wise man's art:
    For folly, that he wisely shows, is fit;
    But wise men, folly-fallen, quite taint their wit.[179]

[*Enter* SIR TOBY BELCH *and* SIR ANDREW AGUECHEEK.]

SIR TOBY. Save you, gentleman.

VIOLA. And you, sir.

SIR ANDREW. *Dieu vous garde, monsieur.*

VIOLA. *Et vous aussi; votre serviteur.*

SIR ANDREW. I hope, sir, you are; and I am yours.

SIR TOBY. Will you encounter the house? my niece is desirous you
should enter, if your trade be to her.

VIOLA. I am bound to your niece, sir: I mean, she is the list[180] of my
voyage.

SIR TOBY. Taste[181] your legs, sir; put them to motion.

VIOLA. My legs do better understand me, sir, than I understand what
you mean by bidding me taste my legs.

SIR TOBY. I mean, to go, sir, to enter.

VIOLA. I will answer you with gait and entrance: but we are
prevented.[182]—

[*Enter* OLIVIA *and* MARIA.]

With cuppe and clapper like a *Lazarous.*

[177] *Element* was constantly in the mouths of those who affected fine talking in the
Poet's time. The intellectual exquisites thus run it into cant. Perhaps the word was as
much overworked as *idea* and *intuition* are in our time.

[178] A *haggard* is a wild or untrained *hawk*, which flies, *checks*, at all birds, or birds
of *every feather*, indiscriminately.

[179] To *taint*, as here used, is to *impeach, attaint*, or bring into an *attainder. Wit*, also,
was used in the sense of *wisdom*, being in fact from the same original.

[180] *List* was often used for *limit* or *boundary*; as, in the well-known language of the
tilting-ground, for *barrier.*

[181] *Taste* was sometimes used in the sense of *try.* So in Chapman's *Odyssey:* "He
now began to *taste* the bow."

[182] *Prevented* in the classical sense of *anticipated* or *forestalled.* Often so.

Most excellent accomplished lady, the heavens rain odours on you!

SIR ANDREW. [*Aside.*] That youth's a rare courtier: *Rain odours*: well.

VIOLA. My matter hath no voice, lady, but to your own most pregnant[183] and vouchsafed car.

SIR ANDREW. [*Aside.*] *Odours, pregnant,* and *vouchsafed*:—I'll get 'em all three ready.

OLIVIA. Let the garden door be shut, and leave me to my hearing. [*Exeunt* SIR TOBY, SIR ANDREW, *and* MARIA.]—Give me your hand, sir.

VIOLA. My duty, madam, and most humble service.

OLIVIA. What is your name?

VIOLA. Cesario is your servant's name, fair princess.

OLIVIA. My servant, sir! 'Twas never merry world,
Since lowly feigning was call'd compliment:
You are servant to the Count Orsino, youth.

VIOLA. And he is yours, and his must needs be yours;
Your servant's servant is your servant, madam.

OLIVIA. For him, I think not on him: for his thoughts,
Would they were blanks rather than fill'd with me!

VIOLA. Madam, I come to whet your gentle thoughts
On his behalf:—

OLIVIA. O, by your leave, I pray you:
I bade you never speak again of him:
But, would you undertake another suit,
I had rather hear you to solicit that
Than music from the spheres.

VIOLA. Dear lady,—

OLIVIA. Give me leave, beseech you: I did send,
After the last enchantment you did here,
A ring in chase of you; so did I abuse
Myself, my servant, and, I fear me, you:
Under your hard construction must I sit;
To force[184] that on you, in a shameful cunning,
Which you knew none of yours. What might you think?
Have you not set mine honour at the stake,
And baited it with all the unmuzzl'd thoughts[185]
That tyrannous heart can think? To one of your
Receiving[186] enough is shown:

---

[183] *Pregnant* here means *apprehensive, quick,* or *intelligent.*

[184] *To force* with the sense of *for forcing.* The Poet abounds in such instances of the infinitive used like the gerund in Latin.

[185] The figure is of a bear or other animal tied to a stake, to be *baited* or *worried* by dogs, with *free* or *unmuzzled* months.

[186] One so quick to *understand* or *apprehend.*

A cyprus,[187] not a bosom, hides my heart.
So, let me hear you speak.
VIOLA. I pity you.
OLIVIA. That's a degree to love.
VIOLA. No, not a grise;[188] for 'tis a vulgar proof
    That very oft we pity enemies.
OLIVIA. Why, then, methinks 'tis time to smile again:
    O world, how apt the poor are to be proud!
    If one should be a prey, how much the better
    To fall before the lion than the wolf! [*Clock strikes.*]
    The clock upbraids me with the waste of time.—
    Be not afraid, good youth, I will not have you:
    And yet, when wit and youth is come to harvest,
    Your wife is like to reap a proper man.
    There lies your way, due-west.
VIOLA. Then westward-ho![189]
    Grace and good disposition 'tend your ladyship!
    You'll nothing, madam, to my lord by me?
OLIVIA. Stay:
    I pr'ythee tell me what thou think'st of me.
VIOLA. That you do think you are not what you are.
OLIVIA. If I think so, I think the same of you.
VIOLA. Then think you right; I am not what I am.
OLIVIA. I would you were as I would have you be!
VIOLA. Would it be better, madam, than I am,
    I wish it might; for now I am your fool.
OLIVIA. O what a deal of scorn looks beautiful
    In the contempt and anger of his lip!
    A murd'rous guilt shows not itself more soon
    Than love that would seem hid: love's night is noon.—
    Cesario, by the roses of the spring,
    By maidhood, honour, truth, and everything,
    I love thee so that, maugre[190] all thy pride,
    Nor wit, nor reason, can my passion hide.
    Do not extort thy reasons from this clause,[191]
    For, that I woo, thou therefore hast no cause:
    But rather reason thus with reason fetter,—

---

[187] *Cyprus* was the name of a light transparent fabric, like lawn.

[188] *Grise* is an old word for *step*, and so means the same as Olivia's *degree*, which is used in the Latin sense.

[189] An exclamation used by watermen on the Thames. *Westward ho, Northward ho,* and *Eastward ho,* were also used as titles of plays.

[190] *Maugre* is *in spite of,* from the French *malgre.*

[191] This is rather darkly expressed; but the meaning appears to be, "Do not, from what I have just said, force or gather reasons for rejecting my offer." Perhaps Olivia thinks her superiority of rank may excuse her in thus making the first open advances.

Love sought is good, but given unsought is better.
VIOLA. By innocence I swear, and by my youth,
    I have one heart, one bosom, and one truth,
    And that no woman has; nor never none[192]
    Shall mistress be of it, save I alone.
    And so adieu, good madam; never more
    Will I my master's tears to you deplore.
OLIVIA. Yet come again: for thou, perhaps, mayst move
    That heart, which now abhors, to like his love. [*Exeunt.*]

SCENE II.

A Room in OLIVIA'*s House.*

[*Enter* SIR TOBY BELCH, SIR ANDREW AGUECHEEK, *and* FABIAN.]

SIR ANDREW. No, faith, I'll not stay a jot longer.
SIR TOBY. Thy reason, dear venom: give thy reason.
FABIAN. You must needs yield your reason, Sir Andrew.
SIR ANDREW. Marry, I saw your niece do more favours to the count's serving-man than ever she bestowed upon me; I saw't i' the orchard.
SIR TOBY. Did she see thee the while, old boy? tell me that.
SIR ANDREW. As plain as I see you now.
FABIAN. This was a great argument of love in her toward you.
SIR ANDREW. 'Slight! will you make an ass o' me?
FABIAN. I will prove it legitimate, sir, upon the oaths of judgment and reason.
SIR TOBY. And they have been grand jurymen since before Noah was a sailor.
FABIAN. She did show favour to the youth in your sight only to exasperate you, to awake your dormouse valour, to put fire in your heart and brimstone in your liver. You should then have accosted her; and with some excellent jests, fire-new from the mint, you should have banged the youth into dumbness. This was looked for at your hand, and this was baulked: the double gilt of this opportunity you let time wash off, and you are now sailed into the north of my lady's opinion; where you will hang like an icicle on Dutchman's beard, unless you do redeem it by some laudable attempt either of valour or policy.

---

[192] We should say, "nor *ever* any." The doubling of negatives is very frequent in Shakespeare, as in all the writers of his time; but such a trebling is rare, at least comparatively so.

SIR ANDREW. And't be any way, it must be with valour: for policy I hate; I had as lief be a Brownist[193] as a politician.

SIR TOBY. Why, then, build me[194] thy fortunes upon the basis of valour. Challenge me the count's youth to fight with him; hurt him in eleven places; my niece shall take note of it: and assure thyself there is no love-broker[195] in the world can more prevail in man's commendation with woman than report of valour.

FABIAN. There is no way but this, Sir Andrew.

SIR ANDREW. Will either of you bear me a challenge to him?

SIR TOBY. Go, write it in a martial hand; be curst[196] and brief; it is no matter how witty, so it be eloquent and full of invention; taunt him with the licence of ink; if thou *thou'st*[197] him some thrice, it shall not be amiss; and as many lies as will lie in thy sheet of paper, although the sheet were big enough for the bed of Ware[198] in England, set 'em down; go about it. Let there be gall enough in thy ink; though thou write with a goose-pen, no matter. About it.

SIR ANDREW. Where shall I find you?

SIR TOBY. We'll call thee at the *cubiculo*:[199] go.

[*Exit* SIR ANDREW.]

FABIAN. This is a dear manikin[200] to you, Sir Toby.

---

[193] The Brownists were one of the radical sects that arose during the reign of Elizabeth; so called from Robert Brown, their founder. Like others of their kind, their leading purpose was to prevent the abuse of certain things, such as laws, by uprooting the use of them. Malvolio appears to have been intended partly as a satire on the Puritans in general; they being especially strenuous at the time this play was written to have restrictions set upon playing. But there had been a deep-seated grudge between the Puritans and the Dramatists ever since Nash put out the eyes of Martin Marprelate with salt.

[194] In colloquial language, *me* was often thus used redundantly, though with a slight dash of humour.

[195] A *love-broker* is one who mediates or *breaks the ice* between two bashful lovers. Pandarus sustains that office in *Troilus and Cressida*; hence our word *pander*.

[196] *Curst* is *cross, snappish*. We should say, "Be *short*," or "Be *tart*."

[197] This has been generally thought an allusion to Coke's abusive *thouing* of Sir Walter Raleigh at his trial; but the play was acted a year and a half before that trial took place. And indeed it had been no insult to *thou* Sir Walter, unless there were some pre-existing custom or sentiment to make it so. What that custom was, may be seen by the following passage from a. book published in 1661, by George Fox the Quaker: "For this *thou* and *thee* was a sore cut to proud flesh, and them that sought self-honour; who, though they would say it to God and Christ, would not endure to have it said to themselves. So that we were often beaten and abused, and sometimes in danger of our lives, for using those words to some proud men, who would say, *What, you ill-bred down, do you* thou *me!*"

[198] This curious piece of furniture was a few years since still in being at one of the inns in that town. It was reported to be twelve feet square, and capable of holding twenty-four persons.

[199] *Cubiculo*, from the Latin *cubiculum*, is a *sleeping-room*.

SIR TOBY. I have been dear to him, lad,—some two thousand strong, or so.[201]

FABIAN. We shall have a rare letter from him: but you'll not deliver it.

SIR TOBY. Never trust me then; and by all means stir on the youth to an answer. I think oxen and wain-ropes cannot hale them together. For Andrew, if he were opened and you find so much blood in his liver[202] as will clog the foot of a flea, I'll eat the rest of the anatomy.

FABIAN. And his opposite, the youth, bears in his visage no great presage of cruelty.

[*Enter* MARIA.]

SIR TOBY. Look where the youngest wren of nine comes.[203]

MARIA. If you desire the spleen,[204] and will laugh yourselves into stitches, follow me: yond gull Malvolio is turned heathen, a very renegado; for there is no Christian, that means to be saved by believing rightly, can ever believe such impossible passages of grossness.[205] He's in yellow stockings.

SIR TOBY. And cross-gartered?

MARIA. Most villainously; like a pedant[206] that keeps a school i' the church.—I have dogged him like his murderer. He does obey every point of the letter that I dropped to betray him. He does smile his face into more lines than is in the new map, with the augmentation of the Indies:[207] you have not seen such a thing as 'tis; I can hardly forbear hurling things at him. I know my lady will strike him; if she do, he'll smile and take't for a great favour.

---

[200] *Manikin* is an old diminutive of *man*; here it means *pet*.

[201] Meaning that he has fooled or dandled so much money out of him.

[202] A red liver, or a liver full of blood, was the common badge of courage, as a white or bloodless liver was of cowardice.

[203] Alluding to the small stature of Maria. Sir Toby elsewhere calls her "the little villain," and Viola ironically speaks of her as "giant." The expression seems to have been proverbial; the *wren* generally laying nine or ten eggs, and the last hatched being the smallest of the brood.

[204] The spleen was held to be the special seat of unbenevolent risibility, and so the cause of teasing or pestering mirth; *splenetic* laughter. Here it seems to mean a fit or turn of excessive merriment, dashed with something of a spiteful humour.

[205] A rather curious commentary on the old notion of "Salvation by orthodoxy," or "belief in believing." The meaning is, that even one who makes a merit of being easy of belief, as thinking to be saved thereby, could not believe a thing so *grossly incredible* as this. The Poet has *impossible* elsewhere in the sense of *incredible*.

[206] The Poet uses *pedant* for *pedagogue*. So Holofernes the schoolmaster is called repeatedly in *Love's Labours Lost*; also the tutors employed for Catharine and Bianca in *The Taming of the Shrew*.

[207] Alluding, no doubt, to a map which appeared in the second edition of Hakluyt's *Voyages*, in 1598. This map is multilineal in the extreme, and is the first in which the Eastern Islands are included.

SIR TOBY. Come, bring us, bring us where he is. [*Exeunt.*]

SCENE III.

A Street.

[*Enter* ANTONIO *and* SEBASTIAN.]

SEBASTIAN. I would not by my will have troubled you;
 But since you make your pleasure of your pains,
 I will no further chide you.
ANTONIO. I could not stay behind you: my desire,
 More sharp than filed steel, did spur me forth;
 And not all love to see you,—though so much,
 As might have drawn one to a longer voyage,—
 But jealousy what might befall your travel,
 Being skilless in these parts; which to a stranger,
 Unguided and unfriended, often prove
 Rough and unhospitable. My willing love,
 The rather by these arguments of fear,
 Set forth in your pursuit.
SEBASTIAN. My kind Antonio,
 I can no other answer make but thanks,
 And thanks, and ever thanks. Often good turns
 Are shuffled off with such uncurrent pay;
 But were my worth,[208] as is my conscience, firm,
 You should find better dealing. What's to do?
 Shall we go see the reliques[209] of this town?
ANTONIO. To-morrow, sir; best, first, go see your lodging.
SEBASTIAN. I am not weary, and 'tis long to night;
 I pray you, let us satisfy our eyes
 With the memorials and the things of fame
 That do renown this city.
ANTONIO. Would you'd pardon me;
 I do not without danger walk these streets:
 Once in a sea-fight, 'gainst the count, his galleys,
 I did some service; of such note, indeed,
 That, were I ta'en here, it would[210] scarce be answered.
SEBASTIAN. Belike you slew great number of his people.

---

[208] *Worth* here stands for *wealth* or *fortune*. Repeatedly so.

[209] *Reliques* for *antiquities*, or, as it is said a little after, "the memorials and the things of fame" that confer renown upon the city.

[210] *Would* for *could*; the auxiliaries *could*, *should*, and *would* being often used indiscriminately. The same with *shall* and *will*; as in a subsequent speech: "Haply your eyes *shall* light," &c.

ANTONIO. The offence is not of such a bloody nature;
　　Albeit the quality of the time and quarrel
　　Might well have given us bloody argument.[211]
　　It might have since been answered in repaying
　　What we took from them; which, for traffic's sake,
　　Most of our city did: only myself stood out;
　　For which, if I be lapsed[212] in this place,
　　I shall pay dear.
SEBASTIAN. Do not then walk too open.
ANTONIO. It doth not fit me. Hold, sir, here's my purse;
　　In the south suburbs, at the Elephant,[213]
　　Is best to lodge: I will bespeak our diet
　　Whiles you beguile the time and feed your knowledge
　　With viewing of the town; there shall you have me.
SEBASTIAN. Why I your purse?
ANTONIO. Haply your eye shall light upon some toy
　　You have desire to purchase; and your store,
　　I think, is not for idle markets, sir.
SEBASTIAN. I'll be your purse-bearer, and leave you for an hour.
ANTONIO. To the Elephant.—
SEBASTIAN. I do remember. [*Exeunt.*]

SCENE IV.

OLIVIA'*s garden.*

[*Enter* OLIVIA *and* MARIA.]

OLIVIA. [*Aside.*] I have sent after him. He says he'll come;
　　How shall I feast him? what bestow on him?[214]
　　For youth is bought more oft than begged or borrowed.
　　I speak too loud.—
　　Where's Malvolio?—he is sad[215] and civil,
　　And suits well for a servant with my fortunes;—
　　Where is Malvolio?

---

[211] *Argument* readily passes over into the sense of *debate*, and *debate* as readily into that of *strife* or *conflict*.

[212] *Lapsed* is, properly, *fallen*; but here carries the sense of making a *slip* or *mis-step*, so as to be recognized and caught.

[213] An inn so named; probably from its having a picture of an elephant for its sign; like the *boar's-head* of Falstaff's famous tavern in Eastcheap. In old times, when but few people could read, *lettered* signs would not do; and so *pictured* ones were used instead.

[214] We should say, "bestow *on* him." This indifferent use of *on* and *of* is very frequent.—In the line before, "says he, he'll come" of course means "*if* he says he'll come." This way of making the subjunctive is common.

[215] *Sad* in its old sense of *serious* or *grave*.

MARIA. He's coming, madam:
   But in very strange manner. He is sure possessed.
OLIVIA. Why, what's the matter? does he rave?
MARIA. No, madam, he does nothing but smile: your ladyship were
   best to have some guard about you if he come; For, sure, the man
   is tainted in his wits.
OLIVIA. Go call him hither.—[*Exit* MARIA.]—I'm as mad as he,
   If sad and merry madness equal be.—

   [*Re-enter* MARIA, *with* MALVOLIO.]

   How now, Malvolio!
MALVOLIO. Sweet lady, ho, ho. [*Smiles fantastically.*]
OLIVIA. Smil'st thou? I sent for thee upon a sad occasion.
MALVOLIO. Sad, lady? I could be sad: this does make some
   obstruction in the blood, this cross-gartering. But what of that? If it
   please the eye of one, it is with me as the very true sonnet is:
   Please one and please all.[216]
OLIVIA. Why, how dost thou, man? what is the matter with thee?
MALVOLIO. Not black in my mind, though yellow in my legs. It did
   come to his hands, and commands shall be executed. I think we do
   know the sweet Roman hand.
OLIVIA. Wilt thou go to bed, Malvolio?
MALVOLIO. To bed? ay, sweetheart; and I'll come to thee.
OLIVIA. God comfort thee! Why dost thou smile so, and kiss thy hand
   so oft?
MARIA. How do you, Malvolio?
MALVOLIO. At your request? Yes; nightingales answer daws.
MARIA. Why appear you with this ridiculous boldness before my
   lady?
MALVOLIO. *Be not afraid of greatness:*—'twas well writ.
OLIVIA. What meanest thou by that, Malvolio?
MALVOLIO. *Some are born great,*—
OLIVIA. Ha?
MALVOLIO.—*some achieve greatness,*—
OLIVIA. What say'st thou?
MALVOLIO.—*And some have greatness thrust upon them.*
OLIVIA. Heaven restore thee!
MALVOLIO. *Remember who commended thy yellow stockings;*—

---

[216] A copy of this "very true sonnet" was discovered a few years ago. It is adorned
with a rude portrait of Queen Elizabeth, with her feathered fan, starched ruff, and ample
farthingale, and is said to have been composed by her Majesty's right merry and facetious
droll, Dick Tarleton; and has the heading, "A prettie new Ballad, intituled, The Crowe
sits upon the wall, Please one and please all." The last line forms the burden, and is
repeated in each stanza.

OLIVIA. Thy yellow stockings?
MALVOLIO.—*and wished to see thee cross-gartered.*
OLIVIA. Cross-gartered?
MALVOLIO. *Go to: thou an made, if thou desirest to be so:*—
OLIVIA. Am I made?
MALVOLIO.—*if not, let me see thee a servant still.*
OLIVIA. Why, this is very midsummer madness.[217]

[*Enter* SERVANT.]

SERVANT. Madam, the young gentleman of the Count Orsino's is returned; I could hardly entreat him back; he attends your ladyship's pleasure.
OLIVIA. I'll come to him. [*Exit* SERVANT.]—Good Maria, let this fellow be looked to. Where's my cousin Toby? Let some of my people have a special care of him; I would not have him miscarry for the half of my dowry.

[*Exeunt* OLIVIA *and* MARIA.]

MALVOLIO. O, ho! do you come near me now? No worse man than Sir Toby to look to me? This concurs directly with the letter: she sends him on purpose, that I may appear stubborn to him; for she incites me to that in the letter. *Cast thy humble slough*, says she;— *be opposite with a kinsman, surly with servants,—let thy tongue tang with arguments of state,—put thyself into the trick of singularity;*—and consequently, sets down the manner how; as, a sad face, a reverend carriage, a slow tongue, in the habit of some sir of note, and so forth. I have limed her;[218] but it is Jove's doing, and Jove make me thankful! And, when she went away now, *Let this fellow be looked to*: Fellow! not Malvolio, nor after my degree, but fellow.[219] Why, everything adheres together; that no dram of a scruple, no scruple of a scruple, no obstacle, no incredulous[220] or unsafe circumstance,—What can be said? Nothing, that can be, can come between me and the full prospect of my hopes. Well, Jove, not I, is the doer of this, and he is to be thanked.

[*Re-enter* MARIA, *with* SIR TOBY BELCH *and* FABIAN.]

---

[217] "'Tis midsummer moon with you" was a proverbial phrase, meaning you are mad. Hot weather was of old thought to affect the brain.

[218] That is, *caught* her, as a bird is caught with lime. *Lime* was used for any *trap* or *snare* for catching birds.

[219] Malvolio takes *fellow* in the sense of *companion* or *equal*.

[220] *Incredulous* for *incredible*; an instance of the indiscriminate use of active and passive forms.

SIR TOBY. Which way is he, in the name of sanctity? If all the Devils of Hell be drawn in little, and Legion himself possessed him, yet I'll speak to him.

FABIAN. Here he is, here he is:—How is't with you, sir? how is't with you, man?

MALVOLIO. Go off; I discard you; let me enjoy my private; go off.

MARIA. Lo, how hollow the fiend speaks within him! did not I tell you?—Sir Toby, my lady prays you to have a care of him.

MALVOLIO. Ah, ha! does she so?

SIR TOBY. Go to, go to; peace, peace, we must deal gently with him; let me alone. How do you, Malvolio? how is't with you? What, man! defy[221] the Devil: consider, he's an enemy to mankind.

MALVOLIO. Do you know what you say?

MARIA. La you, an you speak ill of the Devil, how he takes it at heart! Pray God he be not bewitched.

FABIAN. Carry his water to the wise woman.

MARIA. Marry, and it shall be done to-morrow morning, if I live. My lady would not lose him for more than I'll say.

MALVOLIO. How now, mistress!

MARIA. O lord!

SIR TOBY. Pr'ythee hold thy peace; this is not the way. Do you not see you move him? let me alone with him.

FABIAN. No way but gentleness; gently, gently: the fiend is rough, and will not be roughly used.

SIR TOBY. Why, how now, my bawcock? how dost thou, chuck.[222]

MALVOLIO. Sir?

SIR TOBY. Ay, Biddy,[223] come with me. What, man! 'tis not for gravity to play at cherry-pit with Satan. Hang him, foul collier![224]

MARIA. Get him to say his prayers; good Sir Toby, get him to pray.

MALVOLIO. My prayers, minx?

MARIA. No, I warrant you, he will not hear of godliness.

MALVOLIO. Go, hang yourselves all! you are idle shallow things: I am not of your element; you shall know more hereafter. [*Exit.*]

SIR TOBY. Is't possible?

---

[221] *Defy*, again, for *renounce* or *abjure*.

[222] *Bawcock* and *chuck* were used as terms of playful familiarity, sometimes of endearment.

[223] *Biddy* is a diminutive of *Bridget*. An old term of familiar endearment, applied to chickens and other fowl.

[224] *Cherry-pit* was a game played by pitching cherry-stones into a hole. *Collier* was in Shakespeare's time a term of the highest reproach. The coal-venders were in bad repute, not only from the blackness of their appearance, but that many of them were also great cheats. The Devil is called collier for his blackness. Hence the proverb, "Like will to like, as the *Devil* with the *collier*."

FABIAN. If this were played upon a stage now, I could condemn it as an improbable fiction.

SIR TOBY. His very genius hath taken the infection of the device, man.

MARIA. Nay, pursue him now; lest the device take air and taint.

FABIAN. Why, we shall make him mad indeed.

MARIA. The house will be the quieter.

SIR TOBY. Come, we'll have him in a dark room and bound.[225] My niece is already in the belief that he's mad; we may carry it thus, for our pleasure and his penance, till our very pastime, tired out of breath, prompt us to have mercy on him: at which time we will bring the device to the bar, and crown thee for a finder of madmen. But see, but see.

[*Enter* SIR ANDREW AGUECHEEK.]

FABIAN. More matter for a May morning.[226]

SIR ANDREW. Here's the challenge, read it; I warrant there's vinegar and pepper in't.

FABIAN. Is't so saucy?

SIR ANDREW. Ay, is't, I warrant him; do but read.

SIR TOBY. Give me. [*Reads.*] *Youth, whatsoever thou art, thou art but a scurvy fellow.*

FABIAN. Good and valiant.

SIR TOBY. [*Reads.*] *Wonder not, nor admire not in thy mind, why I do call thee so, for I will show thee no reason for't.*

FABIAN. A good note: that keeps you from the blow of the law.

SIR TOBY. [*Reads.*] *Thou comest to the Lady Olivia, and in my sight she uses thee kindly: but thou liest in thy throat; that is not the matter I challenge thee for.*

FABIAN. Very brief, and to exceeding good sense—less.

SIR TOBY. [*Reads.*] *I will waylay thee going home; where if it be thy chance to kill me,—*

FABIAN. Good.

SIR TOBY. [*Reads.*]*—thou kill'st me like a rogue and a villain.*

FABIAN. Still you keep o' the windy side of the law. Good.

SIR TOBY. [*Reads.*] *Fare thee well; and God have mercy upon one of our souls! He may have mercy upon mine;*[227] *but my hope is better,*

---

[225] This seems to have been the common way of treating madness in the Poet's time.

[226] It was usual on the First of May to exhibit metrical interludes of the comic kind, as well as other sports, such as the Morris-Dance.—In the line before, "a finder of madmen" is probably meant in a legal sense; as when a coroner or jury finds, that is, *brings in* or *renders*, a verdict.

*and so look to thyself. Thy friend, as thou usest him, and thy sworn
enemy,* ANDREW AGUECHEEK.

If this letter move him not, his legs cannot: I'll give't him.

MARIA. You may have very fit occasion for't; he is now in some
commerce with my lady, and will by and by depart.

SIR TOBY. Go, Sir Andrew; scout me for him at the corner of the
orchard, like a bum-baily:[228] so soon as ever thou seest him, draw;
and as thou drawest, swear horrible; for it comes to pass oft that a
terrible oath, with a swaggering accent sharply twanged off, gives
manhood more approbation than ever proof itself would have
earned him. Away.

SIR ANDREW. Nay, let me alone for swearing. [*Exit.*]

SIR TOBY. Now will not I deliver his letter; for the behaviour of the
young gentleman gives him out to be of good capacity and
breeding; his employment between his lord and my niece confirms
no less; therefore this letter, being so excellently ignorant, will
breed no terror in the youth,—he will find it comes from a
clodpole. But, sir, I will deliver his challenge by word of mouth,
set upon Aguecheek notable report of valour, and drive the
gentleman—as I know his youth will aptly receive it,—into a most
hideous opinion of his rage, skill, fury, and impetuosity. This will
so fright them both that they will kill one another by the look, like
cockatrices.[229]

FABIAN. Here he comes with your niece; give them way till he take
leave, and presently after him.

SIR TOBY. I will meditate the while upon some horrid message for a
challenge. [*Exeunt* SIR TOBY, FABIAN, *and* MARIA.]

[*Enter* OLIVIA, *with* VIOLA.]

OLIVIA. I have said too much unto a heart of stone,
And laid mine honour too unchary on it:
There's something in me that reproves my fault;
But such a headstrong potent fault it is
That it but mocks reproof.

VIOLA. With the same 'haviour that your passion bears

---

[227] The man on whose soul he hopes that God will have mercy is the one that he
supposes will fall in the combat: but Sir Andrew hopes to escape unhurt, and to have no
present occasion for that blessing.—MASON.

[228] *Bum-baily* is a waggish form of *bum-bailiff* which, again, is a corruption of
bound-bailiff, a subordinate officer, like our deputy-sheriff, so called from the *bond*
which he had to give for the faithful discharge of his trust.

[229] This imaginary serpent was fabled to have the power of darting venom from its
eyes, or of killing by its look. Shakespeare elsewhere has the phrase, "death-darting eye
of cockatrice." He also has several allusions to the same beast under the name of *basilisk.*

Goes on my master's griefs.

OLIVIA. Here, wear this jewel for me,—'tis my picture;
Refuse it not; it hath no tongue to vex you:
And, I beseech you, come again to-morrow.
What shall you ask of me that I'll deny,
That, honour saved, may upon asking give?

VIOLA. Nothing but this,—your true love for my master.

OLIVIA. How with mine honour may I give him that
Which I have given to you?

VIOLA. I will acquit you.

OLIVIA. Well, come again to-morrow. Fare thee well;
A fiend like thee might bear my soul to Hell. [*Exit.*]

[*Re-enter* SIR TOBY BELCH *and* FABIAN.]

SIR TOBY. Gentleman, God save thee!

VIOLA. And you, sir.

SIR TOBY. That defence thou hast, betake thee to't. Of what nature the
wrongs are thou hast done him, I know not; but thy intercepter, full
of despite, bloody as the hunter, attends thee at the orchard end:
dismount thy tuck, be yare[230] in thy preparation, for thy assailant is
quick, skilful, and deadly.

VIOLA. You mistake, sir; I am sure no man hath any quarrel to me; my
remembrance is very free and clear from any image of offence
done to any man.

SIR TOBY. You'll find it otherwise, I assure you: therefore, if you
hold your life at any price, betake you to your guard; for your
opposite[231] hath in him what youth, strength, skill, and wrath, can
furnish man withal.

VIOLA. I pray you, sir, what is he?

SIR TOBY. He is knight, dubbed with unhacked rapier and on carpet
consideration;[232] but he is a Devil in private brawl; souls and
bodies hath he divorced three; and his incensement at this moment

---

[230] *Tuck* is a rapier or long dagger.—*Yare* is *quick, nimble,* or *prompt.*—"Attends thee" here means *waits for* thee. So in *Coriolanus*, i. 10: "I am *attended* at the cypress grove."

[231] *Opposite* for *opponent* or *adversary*. So in the second scene of this Act: "And his *opposite*, the youth, bears in his visage no great presage of cruelty." Shakespeare never uses *opponent*.

[232] The meaning of this may be gathered from Randle Holme. Speaking of a certain class of knights, he says, "They are termed simply knights of the *carpet*, or knights of the green cloth, to distinguish them from knights that are dubbed as soldiers in the field; though in these days they are created or dubbed with the like ceremony as the others are, by the stroke of a naked sword upon the shoulder."

is so implacable that satisfaction can be none but by pangs of death and sepulchre: hob-nob[233] is his word; give't or take't.

VIOLA. I will return again into the house and desire some conduct[234] of the lady. I am no fighter. I have heard of some kind of men that put quarrels purposely on others to taste[235] their valour: belike this is a man of that quirk.

SIR TOBY. Sir, no; his indignation derives itself out of a very competent injury; therefore, get you on and give him his desire. Back you shall not to the house, unless you undertake that with me which with as much safety you might answer him: therefore on, or strip your sword stark naked; for meddle you must, that's certain, or forswear to wear iron about you.

VIOLA. This is as uncivil as strange. I beseech you, do me this courteous office as to know of the knight what my offence to him is; it is something of my negligence, nothing of my purpose.

SIR TOBY. I Will do so.—Signior Fabian, stay you by this gentleman till my return. [*Exit.*]

VIOLA. Pray you, sir, do you know of this matter?

FABIAN. I know the knight is incensed against you, even to a mortal arbitrement; but nothing of the circumstance more.

VIOLA. I beseech you, what manner of man is he?

FABIAN. Nothing of that wonderful promise, to read him by his form, as you are like to find him in the proof of his valour. He is indeed, sir, the most skilful, bloody, and fatal opposite that you could possibly have found in any part of Illyria. Will you walk towards him? I will make your peace with him if I can.

VIOLA. I shall be much bound to you for't. I am one that would rather go with sir priest than sir knight:[236] I care not who knows so much of my mettle. [*Exeunt.*]

---

[233] *Hob-nob, hab-nab, habbe* or *nabbe*, is *have* or *not have, hit* or *miss.*

[234] *Conduct* for *conductor, escort,* or *convoy.* So in *The Tempest*, v. 1: "There is in this business more than Nature was ever *conduct* of." Also in *The Merchant*, iv, 1: "Go give him courteous *conduct* to this place."

[235] *Taste* in the sense of *try* has occurred before in this Act.

[236] Viola's fright does not quench her humour, or her sense of the ludicrous in her position. Her meaning is, that she would rather be one of the parties in a marriage than in a duel.

SCENE V.

The Street adjoining OLIVIA's *Garden.*

[*Re-enter* SIR TOBY *with* SIR ANDREW.]

SIR TOBY. Why, man, he's a very Devil; I have not seen such a firago.[237] I had a pass with him, rapier, scabbard, and all, and he gives me the stuck-in[238] with such a mortal motion that it is inevitable; and on the answer, he pays you as surely as your feet hit the ground they step on. They say he has been fencer to the Sophy.

SIR ANDREW. Pox on't, I'll not meddle with him.

SIR TOBY. Ay, but he will not now be pacified: Fabian can scarce hold him yonder.

SIR ANDREW. Plague on't; an I thought he had been valiant, and so cunning in fence, I'd have seen him damned ere I'd have challenged him. Let him let the matter slip and I'll give him my horse, gray Capulet.

SIR TOBY. I'll make the motion. Stand here, make a good show on't; this shall end without the perdition of souls.—[*Aside.*] Marry, I'll ride your horse as well as I ride you.—

[*Re-enter* FABIAN *and* VIOLA.]

[*to* FABIAN.] I have his horse to take up[239] the quarrel; I have persuaded him the youth's a Devil.

FABIAN. He is as horribly conceited of him;[240] and pants and looks pale, as if a bear were at his heels.

SIR TOBY. [*to* VIOLA.] There's no remedy, sir: he will fight with you for's oath sake: marry, he hath better bethought him of his quarrel, and he finds that now scarce to be worth talking of: therefore, draw for the supportance of his vow; he protests he will not hurt you.

VIOLA. [*Aside.*] Pray God defend me! A little thing would make me tell them how much I lack of a man.

FABIAN. Give ground if you see him furious.

SIR TOBY. Come, Sir Andrew, there's no remedy; the gentleman will, for his honour's sake, have one bout with you: he cannot by the duello avoid it; but he has promised me, as he is a gentleman and a soldier, he will not hurt you. Come on: to't.

---

[237] *Firago,* for *virago.* The meaning appears to be, "I have never seen a viraginous woman so obstreperous and violent as he is."

[238] A corruption of *stoccata,* an Italian term in fencing.

[239] *Take up* is the old phrase for *make up* or *settle.*

[240] He has as horrid a *conception* of him.

SIR ANDREW. Pray God he keep his oath! [*Draws.*]
VIOLA. I do assure you 'tis against my will. [*Draws.*]

[*Enter* ANTONIO.]

ANTONIO. Put up your sword:—if this young gentleman
     Have done offence, I take the fault on me;
     If you offend him, I for him defy you.
SIR TOBY. You, sir! why, what are you?
ANTONIO. [*Drawing.*] One, sir, that for his love dares yet do more
     Than you have heard him brag to you he will.
SIR TOBY. Nay, if you be an undertaker,[241] I am for you. [*Draws.*]
FABIAN. O good Sir Toby, hold; here come the officers.
SIR TOBY. [*To* ANTONIO.] I'll be with you anon.
VIOLA. [*To* SIR ANDREW.] Pray, sir, put your sword up, if you
     please.
SIR ANDREW. Marry, will I, sir; and for that I promised you, I'll be as
     good as my word. He will bear you easily and reins well.

[*Enter* OFFICERS.]

FIRST OFFICER. This is the man; do thy office.
SECOND OFFICER. Antonio, I arrest thee at the suit
     Of Count Orsino.
ANTONIO. You do mistake me, sir.
FIRST OFFICER. No, sir, no jot; I know your favour well,
     Though now you have no sea-cap on your head.—
     Take him away; he knows I know him well.
ANTONIO. I must obey.—[*To* VIOLA.] This comes with seeking you;
     But there's no remedy; I shall answer it.
     What will you do? Now my necessity
     Makes me to ask you for my purse. It grieves me
     Much more for what I cannot do for you
     Than what befalls myself. You stand amazed;
     But be of comfort.[242]
SECOND OFFICER. Come, sir, away.
ANTONIO. I must entreat of you some of that money.
VIOLA. What money, sir?
     For the fair kindness you have showed me here,
     And part being prompted by your present trouble,
     Out of my lean and low ability

---

[241] One who takes up or *undertakes* the quarrels of others; an intermeddler or intruder.
[242] *Be of comfort* is old language for *be comforted*.

I'll lend you something; my having is not much;
I'll make division of my present with you:
Hold, there is half my coffer.
ANTONIO. Will you deny me now?
Is't possible that my deserts to you
Can lack persuasion? Do not tempt my misery,
Lest that it make me so unsound a man
As to upbraid you with those kindnesses
That I have done for you.
VIOLA. I know of none,
Nor know I you by voice or any feature:
I hate ingratitude more in a man
Than lying, vainness, babbling, drunkenness,
Or any taint of vice whose strong corruption
Inhabits our frail blood.
ANTONIO. O heavens themselves!
SECOND OFFICER. Come, sir, I pray you go.
ANTONIO. Let me speak a little. This youth that you see here
I snatched one half out of the jaws of death,
Relieved him with such sanctity of love,—
And to his image, which methought did promise
Most venerable worth, did I devotion.
FIRST OFFICER. What's that to us? The time goes by; away.
ANTONIO. But O how vile an idol proves this god!
Thou hast, Sebastian, done good feature shame.
In nature there's no blemish but the mind;
None can be call'd deform'd but the unkind:[243]
Virtue is beauty; but the beauteous-evil
Are empty trunks,[244] o'erflourished by the Devil.
FIRST OFFICER. The man grows mad; away with him. Come, come,
sir.
ANTONIO. Lead me on. [*Exeunt* OFFICERS *with* ANTONIO.]
VIOLA. Methinks his words do from such passion fly
That he believes himself; so do not I.[245]
Prove true, imagination; O prove true,
That I, dear brother, be now ta'en for you!
SIR TOBY. Come hither, knight;—come hither, Fabian; we'll whisper
o'er a couplet or two of most sage saws.
VIOLA. He named Sebastian; I my brother know

---

[243] *Unkind*, here, is *unnatural, ungrateful*, or without natural affection. So the Poet often has *kind* for *nature*.

[244] Trunks, being then part of the furniture of apartments, were ornamented with scroll-work or *flourished* devices.

[245] That is, "I do not yet believe myself, when from this accident I gather hope of my brother's life."

Yet living in my glass;[246] even such and so
In favour was my brother; and he went
Still in this fashion, colour, ornament,
For him I imitate. O, if it prove,
Tempests are kind, and salt waves fresh in love! [*Exit.*]

SIR TOBY. A very dishonest paltry boy, and more a coward than a
  hare: his dishonesty appears in leaving his friend here in necessity,
  and denying him; and for his cowardship, ask Fabian.

FABIAN. A coward, a most devout coward, religious in it.

SIR ANDREW. 'Slid, I'll after him again and beat him.

SIR TOBY. Do, cuff him soundly, but never draw thy sword.

SIR ANDREW. And I do not,—[*Exit.*]

FABIAN. Come, let's see the event.

SIR TOBY. I dare lay any money 'twill be nothing yet. [*Exeunt.*]

ACT IV.

SCENE I.

The Street before OLIVIA's *Garden.*

[*Enter* SEBASTIAN *and* CLOWN.]

CLOWN. Will you make me believe that I am not sent for you?

SEBASTIAN. Go to, go to,[247] thou art a foolish fellow;
  Let me be clear of thee.

CLOWN. Well held out, i'faith! No, I do not know you; nor I am not
  sent to you by my lady, to bid you come speak with her; nor your
  name is not Master Cesario; nor this is not my nose neither.
  Nothing that is so is so.

SEBASTIAN. I pr'ythee vent thy folly somewhere else.
  Thou know'st not me.

CLOWN. Vent my folly! he has heard that word of some great man,
  and now applies it to a fool. Vent my folly! I am afraid this great
  lubber, the world, will prove a cockney.[248]—I pr'ythee now, ungird

---

[246] "His resemblance *survives* in the reflection of my own figure."

[247] The phrase *go to*, now pretty much obsolete, was very common in the Poet's time, especially in colloquial language. Sometimes it is nearly equivalent to our *be off*, which appears to be the sense of it in this place; and sometimes it means about the same as *come on*.

[248] The meaning seems to be, "I am afraid this great lumpish world will be all given over to *cockneyism*."—*Cockney* seems to be understood the world over as a term for a Londoner. Minsheu's *Ductor in Linguas*, 1617, explains it thus: "A *Cockney* may be taken for a child tenderly and wantonly brought up." So, too, in Phillips's *World of Words*, 1670: "*Cockney*, a nickname commonly given to one born and bred in the city of London; also a fondling child, tenderly brought up and *cocker'd*."—"Ungird thy

thy strangeness, and tell me what I shall vent to my lady. Shall I vent to her that thou art coming?

SEBASTIAN. I pr'ythee, foolish Greek,[249] depart from me;
There's money for thee; if you tarry longer
I shall give worse payment.

CLOWN. By my troth, thou hast an open hand:—These wise men that give fools money get themselves a good report after fourteen years' purchase.[250]

[*Enter* SIR ANDREW, SIR TOBY, *and* FABIAN.]

SIR ANDREW. Now, sir, have I met you again? there's for you.

[*Striking* SEBASTIAN.]

SEBASTIAN. Why, there's for thee, and there, and there. [*Beating* SIR ANDREW.]
Are all the people mad?

[*Enter* SIR TOBY BELCH, *and* FABIAN.]

SIR TOBY. Hold, sir, or I'll throw your dagger o'er the house.

CLOWN. This will I tell my lady straight. I would not be in some of your coats for twopence. [*Exit.*]

SIR TOBY. Come on, sir; hold. [*Holding* SEBASTIAN.]

SIR ANDREW. Nay, let him alone; I'll go another way to work with him; I'll have an action of battery against him, if there be any law in Illyria: though I struck him first, yet it's no matter for that.

SEBASTIAN. Let go thy hand.

SIR TOBY. Come, sir, I will not let you go. Come, my young soldier, put up your iron: you are well flesh'd;[251] come on.

SEBASTIAN. I will be free from thee. [*Disengages himself.*] What wouldst thou now?
If thou dar'st tempt me further, draw thy sword. [*Draws.*]

---

strangeness" is put off thy estrangement. The Clown, mistaking Sebastian for Cesario, thinks his non-recognition to be put on or assumed.

[249] *A merry Greek*, and *a foolish Greek*, were ancient proverbial expressions applied to boon companions, good fellows, as they were called, who spent their time in riotous mirth.

[250] That is, at a very extravagant price; *twelve* years' purchase being then the current price of estates.

[251] The verb to *flesh* and the noun *fleshment* were used of one's first service with the sword. So, too, an *unfleshed* sword is called a *maiden* sword. Sir Toby means to intimate that Sebastian, whom he supposes to be Viola, is too young to have ever handled that manly weapon before.

SIR TOBY. What, what? Nay, then I must have an ounce or two of this
  malapert blood from you. [*Draws.*]

[*Enter* OLIVIA.]

OLIVIA. Hold, Toby; on thy life, I charge thee hold.
SIR TOBY. Madam?
OLIVIA. Will it be ever thus? Ungracious wretch,
  Fit for the mountains and the barbarous caves,
  Where manners ne'er were preach'd! Out of my sight!
  Be not offended, dear Cesario!—
  Rudesby,[252] be gone!—

[*Exeunt* SIR TOBY, SIR ANDREW, *and* FABIAN.]

      I pr'ythee, gentle friend,
  Let thy fair wisdom, not thy passion, sway
  In this uncivil and unjust extent[253]
  Against thy peace. Go with me to my house,
  And hear thou there how many fruitless pranks
  This ruffian hath botch'd up, that thou thereby
  Mayst smile at this: thou shalt not choose but go;
  Do not deny. Beshrew his soul for me,
  He started one poor heart[254] of mine in thee.
SEBASTIAN. [*Aside.*] What relish is in this? how runs the stream?
  Or I am mad, or else this is a dream:—
  Let fancy still my sense in Lethe steep;
  If it be thus to dream, still let me sleep!
OLIVIA. Nay, come, I pr'ythee. Would thou'dst be ruled by me!
SEBASTIAN. Madam, I will.
OLIVIA. O, say so, and so be! [*Exeunt.*]

---

[252] An old term for *rude fellow*.

[253] *Extent*, as here used, is a legal term for a civil process whereby the person and property of a debtor were seized and held to answer in payment of the debt.

[254] An equivoque is here intended between *hart* and *heart*, which were formerly written alike.

Scene II.

A Room in OLIVIA'*s House.*

[*Enter* MARIA *and the* CLOWN.]

MARIA. Nay, I pr'ythee, put on this gown and this beard; make him believe thou art Sir Topas the curate; do it quickly: I'll call Sir Toby the whilst. [*Exit.*]

CLOWN. Well, I'll put it on, and I will dissemble[255] myself in't; and I would I were the first that ever dissembled in such a gown. I am not tall[256] enough to become the function well: nor lean enough to be thought a good student: but to be said, an honest man and a good housekeeper, goes as fairly as to say, a careful man and a great scholar. The competitors[257] enter.

[*Enter* SIR TOBY BELCH *and* MARIA.]

SIR TOBY. Jove bless thee, Master Parson.

CLOWN. *Bonos dies*, Sir Toby: for as the old hermit of Prague, that never saw pen and ink, very wittily said to a niece of King Gorboduc, *That that is, is*; so I, being master parson, am master parson: for what is *that* but *that*, and *is* but *is*?[258]

SIR TOBY. To him, Sir Topas.

CLOWN. What, hoa, I say,—Peace in this prison!

SIR TOBY. The knave counterfeits well; a good knave.

MALVOLIO. [*Within.*] Who calls there?

CLOWN. Sir Topas the curate, who comes to visit Malvolio the lunatic.

MALVOLIO. [*Within.*] Sir Topas, Sir Topas, good Sir Topas, go to my lady.

CLOWN. Out, hyperbolical fiend![259] how vexest thou this man? talkest thou nothing but of ladies?

---

[255] That is, *disguise*. Shakespeare has here used a Latinism. "*Dissimulo*, to dissemble, to *cloak*, to hide," says Hutton's Dictionary, 1583.

[256] *Tall* was sometimes used in the sense of *lusty*, thus making a good antithesis to *lean*.

[257] *Confederate* or *partner* is one of the old senses of *competitor*.—To be a *good housekeeper* is to be *hospitable*. So, in *2 Henry VI.*, i. 1, we have *housekeeping* for *hospitality*, or *keeping open house*: "Thy deeds, thy plainness, and thy *housekeeping*, have won the greatest favour of the commons."

[258] A humorous banter upon the language of the schools.

[259] This use of *hyperbolical* seems to be original with the Clown. Cowley, however, in his *Essay Of Greatness*, applies the phrase "hyperbolical fop" to one Senecio, who is described by Seneca the Elder as possessed with "a ridiculous affectation of grandeur";

SIR TOBY. Well said, master parson.

MALVOLIO. [*Within.*] Sir Topas, never was man thus wronged: good
Sir Topas, do not think I am mad; they have laid me here in
hideous darkness.

CLOWN. Fie, thou dishonest Satan! I call thee by the most modest
terms; for I am one of those gentle ones that will use the Devil
himself with courtesy. Say'st thou that house is dark?

MALVOLIO. [*Within.*] As Hell, Sir Topas.

CLOWN. Why, it hath bay-windows[260] transparent as barricadoes, and
the clere-storeys[261] toward the south-north are as lustrous as ebony;
and yet complainest thou of obstruction?

MALVOLIO. [*Within.*] I am not mad, Sir Topas; I say to you this
house is dark.

CLOWN. Madman, thou errest. I say there is no darkness but
ignorance; in which thou art more puzzled than the Egyptians in
their fog.

MALVOLIO. [*Within.*] I say this house is as dark as ignorance, though
ignorance were as dark as Hell; and I say there was never man thus
abused. I am no more mad than you are; make the trial of it in any
constant question.[262]

CLOWN. What is the opinion of Pythagoras concerning wild-fowl?

MALVOLIO. [*Within.*] That the soul of our grandam might haply
inhabit a bird.

CLOWN. What thinkest thou of his opinion?

MALVOLIO. [*Within.*] I think nobly of the soul, and no way approve
his opinion.

CLOWN. Fare thee well. Remain thou still in darkness: thou shalt hold
the opinion of Pythagoras ere I will allow of thy wits; and fear to
kill a woodcock,[263] lest thou dispossess the soul of thy grandam.
Fare thee well.

MALVOLIO. [*Within.*] Sir Topas, Sir Topas!

SIR TOBY. My most exquisite Sir Topas!

CLOWN. Nay, I am for all waters.[264]

---

insomuch that he would speak none but big words, eat nothing but what was big, nor
wear any shoe that was not big enough for both his feet.

   [260] *Bay-windows* were large projecting windows, probably so called because they
occupied a whole *bay* or space between two cross-beams in a building.

   [261] *Clere-storeys*, in Gothic architecture, are the row of windows running along the
upper part of a lofty hall or of a church, over the arches of the nave.

   [262] That is, by *repeating the same question*. A crazy man, on being asked to repeat a
thing he has just said, is very apt to go on and say something else. So in *Hamlet*, iii. 4:
"'Tis not madness that I have utter'd: bring me to the test, and I *the matter will re-word*;
which madness would gambol from."

   [263] The Clown mentions a woodcock, because it was proverbial as a foolish bird,
and therefore a proper ancestor for a man out of his wits.

   [264] The meaning appears to be, I can turn my hand to any thing, or assume any
character. Florio in his translation of Montaigne, speaking of Aristotle, says, "He hath *an*

MARIA. Thou mightst have done this without thy beard and gown: he sees thee not.

SIR TOBY. To him in thine own voice, and bring me word how thou findest him; I would we were well rid of this knavery. If he may be conveniently delivered, I would he were; for I am now so far in offence with my niece that I cannot pursue with any safety this sport to the upshot. Come by and by to my chamber. [*Exeunt* SIR TOBY *and* MARIA.]

CLOWN. [*Singing.*]

> *Hey, Robin, jolly Robin,*
> *Tell me how thy lady does.*[265]

MALVOLIO. [*Within.*] Fool,—

CLOWN. [*Singing.*]

> *My lady is unkind, perdy.*

MALVOLIO. [*Within.*] Fool,—

CLOWN. [*Singing.*]

> *Alas, why is she so?*

MALVOLIO. [*Within.*] Fool, I say;—

CLOWN. [*Singing.*]

> *She loves another*—Who calls, ha?

MALVOLIO. [*Within.*] Good fool, as ever thou wilt deserve well at my hand, help me to a candle, and pen, ink, and paper; as I am a gentleman, I will live to be thankful to thee for't.

CLOWN. Master Malvolio!

MALVOLIO. [*Within.*] Ay, good fool.

CLOWN. Alas, sir, how fell you besides your five wits?

MALVOLIO. [*Within.*] Fool, there was never man so notoriously[266] abused; I am as well in my wits, fool, as thou art.

CLOWN. But as well? then you are mad indeed, if you be no better in your wits than a fool.

---

oar in every water, and meddleth with all things." And in his *Second Frutes*: "I am a knight for *all saddles.*"

[265] This ballad may be found in Percy's *Reliques.* Dr. Nott has also printed it among the poems of Sir Thomas Wyatt the elder.

[266] *Notoriously* in the sense of *prodigiously* or *outrageously.* We have *notorious* in the same sense near the end of the play.

MALVOLIO. [*Within.*] They have here propertied me;[267] keep me in darkness, send ministers to me, asses, and do all they can to face me out of my wits.

CLOWN. Advise you what you say: the minister is here.[268]—[*As* SIR TOPAS.] Malvolio, thy wits the heavens restore! endeavour thyself to sleep, and leave thy vain bibble-babble.

MALVOLIO. [*Within.*] Sir Topas,—

CLOWN. Maintain no words with him, good fellow.—Who, I, sir? Not I, sir. God b' wi' you,[269] good Sir Topas.—Marry, amen.—I will sir, I will.

MALVOLIO. [*Within.*] Fool, fool, fool, I say,—

CLOWN. Alas, sir, be patient. What say you, sir? I am shent[270] for speaking to you.

MALVOLIO. [*Within.*] Good fool, help me to some light and some paper;
I tell thee I am as well in my wits as any man in Illyria.

CLOWN. Well-a-day,—that you were, sir!

MALVOLIO. [*Within.*] By this hand, I am: Good fool, some ink, paper, and light, and convey what I will set down to my lady; it shall advantage thee more than ever the bearing of letter did.

CLOWN. I will help you to't. But tell me true, are you not mad indeed? or do you but counterfeit?

MALVOLIO. [*Within.*] Believe me, I am not; I tell thee true.

CLOWN. Nay, I'll ne'er believe a madman till I see his brains.
I will fetch you light, and paper, and ink.

MALVOLIO. [*Within.*] Fool, I'll requite it in the highest degree: I pr'ythee be gone.

CLOWN. [*Singing.*]

> *I am gone, sir, and anon, sir,*
> *I'll be with you again,*
> *In a trice, like to the old Vice,*[271]

---

[267] "Taken possession of me as of a man unable to look to himself."

[268] The Clown, in the dark, acts two persons, and counterfeits, by variation of voice, a dialogue between himself and Sir Topas; the preceding part of this speech being spoken as Clown, the following as Priest.—"*Advise* you" is *bethink* you, *consider*, or *be careful*.—In the next line, "endeavour thyself to sleep" is *induce*, *persuade*, or *compose* thyself; *endeavour* being used transitively.

[269] Here we have the old phrase "God be with you" in the process of contraction into the modern phrase *good bye*.

[270] *Shent* is an old word for *scolded*, *blamed*, or *reprimanded*.

[271] Both the Vice and the Devil were stereotyped personages in the old Moral-plays which were in use for many' ages before the Poet's time, and were then just going out of use. The Vice, sometimes called Iniquity, was grotesquely dressed in a cap with ass's ears, and a long coat, and armed with a dagger of lath. He commonly acted the part of a broad, rampant jester and buffoon, full of mad pranks and mischief-making, liberally dashed with a sort of tumultuous, swaggering fun. Especially, he was given to cracking

Your need to sustain;

Who with dagger of lath, in his rage and his wrath,
   Cries ah, ha! to the Devil:
Like a mad lad, Pare thy nails, dad.
   Adieu, goodman[272] *drivel. [Exit.]*

SCENE III.

OLIVIA's *Garden.*

[*Enter* SEBASTIAN.]

SEBASTIAN. This is the air; that is the glorious sun;
   This pearl she gave me, I do feel't and see't:
   And though 'tis wonder that enwraps me thus,
   Yet 'tis not madness. Where's Antonio, then?
   I could not find him at the Elephant;
   Yet there he was; and there I found this credit,[273]
   That he did range the town to seek me out.
   His counsel now might do me golden service;
   For though my soul disputes well with my sense,
   That this may be some error, but no madness,
   Yet doth this accident and flood of fortune
   So far exceed all instance, all discourse,
   That I am ready to distrust mine eyes
   And wrangle with my reason, that persuades me
   To any other trust but that I am mad,—
   Or else the lady's mad; yet if 'twere so,
   She could not sway her house, command her followers,
   Take and give back affairs and their dispatch,[274]

---

ribald and saucy jokes with and upon the Devil, and treating him with a style of coarse familiarity and mockery; and a part of his ordinary functions was to bestride the Devil, and beat him with his dagger till he roared, and the audience roared with him; the scene ending with his being carried off to Hell on the Devil's back. The Vice was the germ of the professional Fool or Clown, which Shakespeare delivers in so many forms, and always so full of matter.

[272] *Goodman* in old language is nearly equivalent to *master*, or to our flattened form of it, *mister*. It was common for women to speak of their husbands as *my goodman*. And in St. Matthew, XX. II: "They murmured against the *goodman* of the house." Also in St. Luke, xii. 39. The verses in the text are most likely from an old popular song, of which nothing further is known.

[273] *Credit* is oddly used here, but in the sense, apparently, of *information* or *intelligence*. So in a letter from Queen Elizabeth to Sir Nicholas Throckmorton: "This bearer came from you with great speed. We have heard his *credit*, and find your carefulness and diligence very great."

With such a smooth, discreet, and stable bearing,
As I perceive she does: there's something in't
That is deceivable.[275] But here comes the lady.

[*Enter* OLIVIA *and a* PRIEST.]

OLIVIA. Blame not this haste of mine. If you mean well,
　　Now go with me and with this holy man
　　Into the chantry[276] by: there, before him
　　And underneath that consecrated roof,
　　Plight me the full assurance of your faith,
　　That my most jealous and too doubtful[277] soul
　　May live at peace. He shall conceal it
　　Whiles you are willing it shall come to note,[278]
　　What time we will our celebration keep
　　According to my birth.—What do you say?
SEBASTIAN. I'll follow this good man, and go with you;
　　And, having sworn truth, ever will be true.
OLIVIA. Then lead the way, good father;—And heavens so shine
　　That they may fairly note this act of mine![279] [*Exeunt.*]

---

[274] The language is very odd and obscure, and gives but a slight hint of the speaker's probable meaning. A good housekeeper, at the head of a large domestic establishment, naturally has her time a good deal occupied in taking account or receiving word of things that need to be done, and in issuing orders and directions for the doing of them, or for "their dispatch."

[275] *Deceivable* for *deceiving* or *deceptive*; the passive form, again, with the active sense.

[276] A *chantry* was a little chapel, or particular altar in some cathedral or parochial church, endowed for the purpose of having Masses sung therein for the souls of the founders; a place for *chanting*.

[277] *Doubtful* in the sense of *fearful*. The Poet often uses *doubt* for *fear*.

[278] *Whiles* was often used thus in the sense of *until.*—*Note*, from the Latin *notitia*, is several times used by the Poet in the sense of *knowledge.*—The ceremony to which Olivia here so sweetly urges Sebastian is the ancient solemn troth-plight, as it was called, which, as it had the binding force of an actual marriage, might well give peace to an anxious maiden till the day of full nuptial possession should arrive.

[279] A bright, glad sunshine falling upon a bride or new-made wife was formerly thought auspicious; it inspired a feeling that the Powers above were indeed smiling their benediction upon the act; and so was fitting cause for prayer beforehand, and of thanksgiving afterwards. Of course this was a fond old superstition: but I believe marriage is not even yet so far enlightened and "de-religionized" but that something of the old feeling still survives.

ACT V.

SCENE I.

The Street before OLIVIA'*s House.*

[*Enter the* CLOWN *and* FABIAN.]

FABIAN. Now, as thou lovest me, let me see his letter.

CLOWN. Good Master Fabian, grant me another request.

FABIAN. Anything.

CLOWN. Do not desire to see this letter.

FABIAN. This is to give a dog; and in recompense desire my dog again.

[*Enter* DUKE, VIOLA, CURIO, *and* ATTENDANTS.]

DUKE. Belong you to the Lady Olivia, friends?

CLOWN. Ay, sir; we are some of her trappings.

DUKE. I know thee well. How dost thou, my good fellow?

CLOWN. Truly, sir, the better for my foes and the worse for my friends.

DUKE. Just the contrary; the better for thy friends.

CLOWN. No, sir, the worse.

DUKE. How can that be?

CLOWN. Marry, sir, they praise me and make an ass of me; now my foes tell me plainly I am an ass: so that by my foes, sir, I profit in the knowledge of myself, and by my friends I am abused: so that, conclusions to be as kisses,[280] if your four negatives make your two affirmatives, why then, the worse for my friends and the better for my foes.

DUKE. Why, this is excellent.

CLOWN. By my troth, sir, no; though it please you to be one of my friends.

---

[280] Warburton thought this should be, "conclusion to be asked is"; upon which Coleridge remarks thus: "Surely Warburton could never have wooed by kisses and won, or he would not have flounder-flatted so just and humorous, nor less pleasing than humorous, an image into so profound a nihility. In the name of love and wonder, do not four kisses make a double affirmative? The humour lies in the whispered 'No!' and the inviting 'Don't!' with which the maiden's kisses are accompanied, and thence compared to negatives, which by repetition constitute an affirmative." The Cambridge Editors, however, note upon the passage thus: "The meaning seems to be nothing more recondite than this: as in the syllogism it takes two premises to make one conclusion, so it takes two people to make one kiss."

DUKE. Thou shalt not be the worse for me; there's gold. [*Gives money.*]

CLOWN. But that it would be double-dealing, sir, I would you could make it another.

DUKE. O, you give me ill counsel.

CLOWN. Put your grace in your pocket,[281] sir, for this once, and let your flesh and blood obey it.

DUKE. Well, I will be so much a sinner to be a double-dealer: there's another. [*Gives money.*]

CLOWN. *Primo, secundo, tertio,* is a good play; and the old saying is, the third pays for all; the *triplex,* sir, is a good tripping measure; or the bells of Saint Bennet, sir, may put you in mind,—one, two, three.

DUKE. You can fool no more money out of me at this throw: if you will let your lady know I am here to speak with her, and bring her along with you, it may awake my bounty further.

CLOWN. Marry, sir, lullaby to your bounty till I come again. I go, sir; but I would not have you to think that my desire of having is the sin of covetousness: but, as you say, sir, let your bounty take a nap; I will awake it anon. [*Exit.*]

[*Enter* OFFICERS, with ANTONIO.]

VIOLA. Here comes the man, sir, that did rescue me.

DUKE. That face of his I do remember well:
    Yet when I saw it last it was besmeared
    As black as Vulcan in the smoke of war:
    A bawbling vessel was he captain of,
    For shallow draught and bulk unprizable;[282]
    With which such scathful grapple did he make
    With the most noble bottom of our fleet
    That very envy and the tongue of loss[283]
    Cried fame and honour on him.—What's the matter?

FIRST OFFICER. Orsino, this is that Antonio
    That took the Phoenix and her fraught from Candy:
    And this is he that did the *Tiger* board
    When your young nephew Titus lost his leg:
    Here in the streets, desperate of shame and state,[284]

---

[281] The Clown puns so swiftly here that it is not easy to keep up with him. The quibble lies between the two senses of *grace* as a title and as a gracious impulse or thought.

[282] *Unprizable* is evidently used here in the sense of *worthless,* or of *no price.* The Poet elsewhere has it in the opposite sense of *inestimable.*

[283] "The tongue of *loss*" here means the tongue of the *loser;* but is much more elegant.—*Scathful* is *harmful, damaging,* or *destructive.*

In private brabble did we apprehend him.

VIOLA. He did me kindness, sir; drew on my side;
But, in conclusion, put strange speech upon me,—
I know not what 'twas, but distraction.

DUKE. Notable pirate! thou salt-water thief!
What foolish boldness brought thee to their mercies,
Whom thou, in terms so bloody and so dear,[285]
Hast made thine enemies?

ANTONIO. Orsino, noble sir,
Be pleased that I shake off these names you give me:
Antonio never yet was thief or pirate,
Though, I confess, on base and ground enough,
Orsino's enemy. A witchcraft drew me hither:
That most ingrateful boy there, by your side
From the rude sea's enraged and foamy mouth
Did I redeem; a wreck past hope he was:
His life I gave him, and did thereto add
My love, without retention or restraint,
All his in dedication: for his sake,
Did I expose myself, pure for his love,
Into the danger of this adverse town;
Drew to defend him when he was beset:
Where being apprehended, his false cunning,—
Not meaning to partake with me in danger,—
Taught him to face me out of his acquaintance,
And grew a twenty-years-removed thing
While one would wink; denied me mine own purse,
Which I had recommended to his use
Not half an hour before.

VIOLA. How can this be?

DUKE. When came he to this town?

ANTONIO. To-day, my lord; and for three months before,—
No interim, not a minute's vacancy,—
Both day and night did we keep company.

DUKE. Here comes the countess; now Heaven walks on earth.—
But for thee, fellow, fellow, thy words are madness:
Three months this youth hath tended upon me;
But more of that anon.—Take him aside.

---

[284] Inattentive to his character or condition, like a desperate man.

[285] *Dear* is used in the same sense here as in *Hamlet*: "Would I had met my *dearest* foe in Heaven!" Tooke has shown that this is much nearer the original sense of the word than the meaning commonly put upon it; dear being from the Anglo-Saxon verb to *dere*, which signifies to hurt. An object of love, any thing that we hold dear, may obviously cause us pain, distress, or solicitude: hence the word came to be used in the opposite senses of hateful and beloved.

[*Enter* OLIVIA *and* ATTENDANTS.]

OLIVIA. What would my lord, but that he may not have,
    Wherein Olivia may seem serviceable?—
    Cesario, you do not keep promise with me.
VIOLA. Madam?
DUKE. Gracious Olivia,—
OLIVIA. What do you say, Cesario?—Good my lord,—
VIOLA. My lord would speak, my duty hushes me.
OLIVIA. If it be aught to the old tune, my lord,
    It is as fat and fulsome[286] to mine ear
    As howling after music.
DUKE. Still so cruel?
OLIVIA. Still so constant, lord.
DUKE. What! to perverseness? you uncivil lady,
    To whose ingrate and unauspicious altars
    My soul the faithfull'st offerings hath breathed out
    That e'er devotion tender'd! What shall I do?
OLIVIA. Even what it please my lord, that shall become him.
DUKE. Why should I not, had I the heart to do it.
    Like to the Egyptian thief, at point of death,
    Kill what I love?[287] a savage jealousy
    That sometime savours nobly.—But hear me this:
    Since you to non-regardance cast my faith,
    And that I partly know the instrument
    That screws me from my true place in your favour,
    Live you the marble-breasted tyrant still;
    But this your minion, whom I know you love,
    And whom, by Heaven I swear, I tender dearly,
    Him will I tear out of that cruel eye
    Where he sits crowned in his master's spite.—
    Come, boy, with me; my thoughts are ripe in mischief:
    I'll sacrifice the lamb that I do love,

---

[286] Both *fat* and *fulsome* seem here to have nearly the sense of *dull, gross*, or *sickening*. The Poet uses *fulsome* of a wine that soon palls upon the taste from its excessive sweetness.

[287] An allusion to the story of Thyamis, as told by Heliodorus in his *Ethiopics*, of which an English version by Thomas Underdowne was published a second time in 1587. Thyamis was a native of Memphis, and chief of a band of robbers. Chariclea, a Greek, having fallen into his hands, he grew passionately in love with her, and would have married her; but, being surprised by a stronger band of robbers, and knowing he must die, he went to the cave where he had secreted her with his other treasures, and, seizing her by the hair with his left hand, with his right plunged a sword in her breast; it being the custom with those barbarians, when they despaired of their own life, first to kill those whom they held most dear, so as to have them as companions in the other world.

To spite a raven's heart within a dove. [*Going.*]
VIOLA. And I, most jocund, apt, and willingly,
    To do you rest, a thousand deaths would die. [*Following.*]
OLIVIA. Where goes Cesario?
VIOLA. After him I love
    More than I love these eyes, more than my life,
    More, by all mores, than e'er I shall love wife.—
    If I do feign, you witnesses above
    Punish my life for tainting of my love!
OLIVIA. Ah me, detested! how am I beguil'd!
VIOLA. Who does beguile you? who does do you wrong?
OLIVIA. Hast thou forgot thyself? Is it so long?—
    Call forth the holy father. [*Exit an* ATTENDANT.]
DUKE. [*To* VIOLA.] Come, away!
OLIVIA. Whither, my lord? Cesario, husband, stay.
DUKE. Husband?
OLIVIA. Ay, husband, can he that deny?
DUKE. [*To* VIOLA.] Her husband, sirrah?
VIOLA. No, my lord, not I.
OLIVIA. Alas, it is the baseness of thy fear
    That makes thee strangle thy propriety:[288]
    Fear not, Cesario, take thy fortunes up;
    Be that thou know'st thou art, and then thou art
    As great as that thou fear'st.—

[*Re-enter* ATTENDANT, *with the* PRIEST.]

      O, welcome, father!
    Father, I charge thee, by thy reverence,
    Here to unfold,—though lately we intended
    To keep in darkness what occasion now
    Reveals before 'tis ripe,—what thou dost know
    Hath newly passed between this youth and me.
PRIEST. A contract of eternal bond of love,
    Confirmed by mutual joinder of your hands,
    Attested by the holy close of lips,
    Strengthen'd by interchangement of your rings;[289]
    And all the ceremony of this compact
    Sealed in my function, by my testimony:
    Since when, my watch hath told me, toward my grave,
    I have travelled but two hours.
DUKE. O thou dissembling cub! What wilt thou be,

---

[288] "Suppress or disown thy *proper* self; deny what you really are."
[289] In ancient espousals the man received as well as gave a ring.

When time hath sowed a grizzle on thy case?[290]
Or will not else thy craft so quickly grow
That thine own trip shall be thine overthrow?
Farewell, and take her; but direct thy feet
Where thou and I henceforth may never meet.
VIOLA. My lord, I do protest,—
OLIVIA. O, do not swear;
Hold little faith, though thou has too much fear.

[*Enter* SIR ANDREW AGUECHEEK, *with his head broken.*]

SIR ANDREW. For the love of God, a surgeon; send one presently to
Sir Toby.
OLIVIA. What's the matter?
SIR ANDREW. 'Has broke my head across, and has given Sir Toby a
bloody coxcomb too: for the love of God, your help: I had rather
than forty pound I were at home.
OLIVIA. Who has done this, Sir Andrew?
SIR ANDREW. The Count's gentleman, one Cesario: we took him for
a coward, but he's the very Devil incardinate.
DUKE. My gentleman, Cesario?
SIR ANDREW. 'Od's lifelings,[291] here he is!—You broke my head for
nothing; and that that I did, I was set on to do't by Sir Toby.
VIOLA. Why do you speak to me? I never hurt you:
You drew your sword upon me without cause;
But I bespake you fair and hurt you not.
SIR ANDREW. If a bloody coxcomb be a hurt, you have hurt me; I
think you set nothing by a bloody coxcomb.—Here comes Sir
Toby halting,—you shall hear more: but if he had not been in drink
he would have tickled you othergates[292] than he did.

[*Enter* SIR TOBY BELCH, *led by the* CLOWN.]

DUKE. How now, gentleman? how is't with you?
SIR TOBY. That's all one: 'has hurt me, and there's the end on't.—
Sot, didst see Dick Surgeon, sot?

---

[290] The skin of a fox or rabbit was often called its case. So in Cary's *Present State of
England*, 1626: "Queen Elizabeth asked a knight, named Young, how he liked a company
of brave ladies. He answered, "As I like my silver-haired conies at home: the *cases* are
far better than the bodies."

[291] *Lifelings* is a diminutive of *life*, as *pittikins* is of *pity*. '*Od's* is one of the
disguised oaths so common in old colloquial language; the original form being *God's*.
We have Imogen exclaiming '*Od's pittikins* in *Cymbeline*, iv. 2.

[292] *Othergates* is an old word meaning the same as our *otherwise*.

CLOWN. O, he's drunk, Sir Toby, an hour agone; his eyes were set at eight i' the morning.

SIR TOBY. Then he's a rogue. After a passy-measures paynim:[293] I hate a drunken rogue.

OLIVIA. Away with him. Who hath made this havoc with them?

SIR ANDREW. I'll help you, Sir Toby, because we'll be dressed together.

SIR TOBY. Will you help an ass-head, and a coxcomb, and a knave? A thin-faced knave, a gull?

OLIVIA. Get him to bed, and let his hurt be looked to.

[*Exeunt* CLOWN, SIR TOBY, *and* SIR ANDREW.]

[*Enter* SEBASTIAN.]

SEBASTIAN. I am sorry, madam, I have hurt your kinsman;
But, had it been the brother of my blood,
I must have done no less, with wit and safety.
You throw a strange regard[294] upon me, and by that
I do perceive it hath offended you;
Pardon me, sweet one, even for the vows
We made each other but so late ago.

DUKE. One face, one voice, one habit, and two persons;
A natural perspective,[295] that is, and is not.

SEBASTIAN. Antonio, O my dear Antonio!
How have the hours rack'd and tortur'd me
Since I have lost thee.

ANTONIO. Sebastian are you?

SEBASTIAN. Fear'st thou that, Antonio?

ANTONIO. How have you made division of yourself?—
An apple, cleft in two, is not more twin
Than these two creatures. Which is Sebastian?

OLIVIA. Most wonderful!

SEBASTIAN. Do I stand there? I never had a brother:
Nor can there be that deity in my nature
Of here and everywhere. I had a sister
Whom the blind waves and surges have devoured:—

---

[293] *Paynim*, meaning *pagan* or *heathen*, was of old a common term of reproach. Sir Toby is too deeply fuddled to have his tongue in firm keeping, and so uses *passy-measures* for *past-measure*, probably.

[294] A *strange regard* is a *look of estrangement* or *alienation*.

[295] A *perspective* formerly meant a glass that assisted the sight in any way. The several kinds used in Shakespeare's time are enumerated in Scot's *Discoverie of Witchcraft*, 1584, where that alluded to by the Duke is thus described: "There his glasses also wherein one man may see another man's image and not his own,"—where that which is, is not; or appears, in a different position, another thing.

[*To* VIOLA.] Of charity, what kin are you to me?
What countryman, what name, what parentage?
VIOLA. Of Messaline: Sebastian was my father;
Such a Sebastian was my brother too:
So went he suited to his watery tomb:
If spirits can assume both form and suit,
You come to fright us.
SEBASTIAN. A spirit I am indeed:
But am in that dimension grossly clad,
Which from the womb I did participate.
Were you a woman, as the rest goes even,
I should my tears let fall upon your cheek,
And say, *Thrice welcome, drowned Viola!*
VIOLA. My father had a mole upon his brow,—
SEBASTIAN. And so had mine.
VIOLA.—And died that day when Viola from her birth
Had numbered thirteen years.
SEBASTIAN. O, that record is lively in my soul!
He finished, indeed, his mortal act
That day that made my sister thirteen years.
VIOLA. If nothing lets[296] to make us happy both
But this my masculine usurp'd attire,
Do not embrace me till each circumstance
Of place, time, fortune, do cohere, and jump,[297]
That I am Viola: which to confirm,
I'll bring you to a captain in this town,
Where lie my maiden weeds; by whose gentle help
I was preferr'd[298] to serve this noble count;
All the occurrence of my fortune since
Hath been between this lady and this lord.
SEBASTIAN. [*To* OLIVIA.] So comes it, lady, you have been
mistook:
But nature to her bias drew in that.[299]
You would have been contracted to a maid;
Nor are you therein, by my life, deceived;
You are betroth'd both to a maid and man.[300]

---

[296] *Let*, often used in the English Bible, but now obsolete, is an old word for *hinder* or *prevent*.

[297] The Poet repeatedly has *jump* in the sense of *agree* or *accord*.

[298] *Prefer* was often used in the sense of *recommend*.

[299] To be *mistook* was sometimes used, as to be *mistaken* now is, in the sense of *making a mistake*. The mistake Olivia has made is in being betrothed to Sebastian instead of Viola; but this was owing to the bias or predisposition of Nature, who would not have a woman betrothed to a woman.

[300] Sebastian applies the term *maid* apparently to himself, in the sense of *virgin*. And why not *maiden man* as well as *maiden sword* or *maiden speeeh*?

DUKE. Be not amazed; right noble is his blood.—
    If this be so, as yet the glass seems true,
    I shall have share in this most happy wreck.—
    [*To* VIOLA.] Boy, thou hast said to me a thousand times,
    Thou never shouldst love woman like to me.
VIOLA. And all those sayings will I over-swear;
    And all those swearings keep as true in soul
    As doth that orbed continent[301] the fire
    That severs day from night.
DUKE. Give me thy hand;
    And let me see thee in thy woman's weeds.
VIOLA. The captain that did bring me first on shore
    Hath my maid's garments: he, upon some action,
    Is now in durance, at Malvolio's suit;
    A gentleman and follower of my lady's.
OLIVIA. He shall enlarge him:—fetch Malvolio hither:—
    And yet, alas, now I remember me,
    They say, poor gentleman, he's much distraught.

[*Re-enter the* CLOWN *with a letter, and* FABIAN.]

A most extracting frenzy of mine own
    From my remembrance clearly banish'd his.—
    How does he, sirrah?
CLOWN. Truly, madam, he holds Beelzebub at the stave's end as well
    as a man in his case may do. 'Has here writ a letter to you; I should
    have given it you to-day morning, but as a madman's epistles are
    no gospels, so it skills not much[302] when they are deliver'd.
OLIVIA. Open it, and read it.
CLOWN. Look then to be well edified when the Fool delivers the
    madman. [*Reads.*] *By the Lord, madam,*—
OLIVIA. How now! art thou mad?
CLOWN. No, madam, I do but read madness: an your ladyship will
    have it as it ought to be, you must allow *vox.*[303]
OLIVIA. Pr'ythee, read i' thy right wits.
CLOWN. So I do, madonna; but to read his right wits is to read thus;
    therefore perpend,[304] my princess, and give ear.
OLIVIA. [*To* FABIAN.] Read it you, sirrah.
FABIAN. [*Reads.*] *By the Lord, madam, you wrong me, and the world*
    shall know it: though you have put me into darkness and given

---

[301] *Continent* formerly meant any thing that *contains.*

[302] A common phrase in the Poet's time, meaning *it signifies not much.*

[303] If you would have the letter read in character, you must allow me to assume the
voice or frantic tone of a madman."

[304] *Perpend* is *consider* or *weigh.*

your drunken cousin rule over me, yet have I the benefit of my senses as well as your ladyship. I have your own letter that induced me to the semblance I put on; with the which I doubt not but to do myself much right or you much shame. Think of me as you please. I leave my duty a little unthought of, and speak out of my injury.

THE MADLY-USED MALVOLIO

OLIVIA. Did he write this?

CLOWN. Ay, madam.

DUKE. This savours not much of distraction.

OLIVIA. See him delivered, Fabian: bring him hither.—

[*Exit* FABIAN.]

My lord, so please you, these things further thought on,
To think me as well a sister as a wife,
One day shall crown the alliance on't, so please you,
Here at my house, and at my proper cost.

DUKE. Madam, I am most apt to embrace your offer.—
[*to* VIOLA.] Your master quits you;[305] and, for your service done him,
So much against the mettle of your sex,
So far beneath your soft and tender breeding,
And since you called me master for so long,
Here is my hand; you shall from this time be
You master's mistress.

OLIVIA. A sister!—you are she.

[*Re-enter* FABIAN *with* MALVOLIO.]

DUKE. Is this the madman?

OLIVIA. Ay, my lord, this same.—
How now, Malvolio!

MALVOLIO. Madam, you have done me wrong,
Notorious wrong.

OLIVIA. Have I, Malvolio? no.

MALVOLIO. Lady, you have. Pray you peruse that letter:
You must not now deny it is your hand,—
Write from it,[306] if you can, in hand or phrase;
Or say 'tis not your seal, not your invention:
You can say none of this. Well, grant it then,

---

[305] *Quit* for *acquit*, and in the sense of *release, discharge,* or *set free.* So in *Henry V.*, iii. 4: "For your great seats, now *quit* you of great shames."

[306] Write *differently* from it. We have similar phraseology in common use; as, "His speaking was from the purpose."

And tell me, in the modesty of honour,
Why you have given me such clear lights of favour;
Bade me come smiling and cross-garter'd to you;
To put on yellow stockings, and to frown
Upon Sir Toby and the lighter people:
And, acting this in an obedient hope,
Why have you suffer'd me to be imprison'd,
Kept in a dark house, visited by the priest,
And made the most notorious geck[307] and gull
That e'er invention played on? tell me why.

OLIVIA. Alas, Malvolio, this is not my writing,
Though, I confess, much like the character:
But out of question, 'tis Maria's hand.
And now I do bethink me, it was she
First told me thou wast mad; then cam'st in smiling,
And in such forms which here were presuppos'd
Upon thee in the letter. Pr'ythee, be content:
This practice hath most shrewdly pass'd upon thee:
But, when we know the grounds and authors of it,
Thou shalt be both the plaintiff and the judge
Of thine own cause.

FABIAN. Good madam, hear me speak;
And let no quarrel, nor no brawl to come,
Taint the condition of this present hour,
Which I have wonder'd at. In hope it shall not,
Most freely I confess, myself and Toby
Set this device against Malvolio here,
Upon some stubborn and uncourteous parts
We had conceiv'd against him. Maria writ
The letter, at Sir Toby's great importance;[308]
In recompense whereof he hath married her.
How with a sportful malice it was follow'd
May rather pluck on laughter than revenge,
If that the injuries be justly weigh'd
That have on both sides pass'd.

OLIVIA. Alas, poor fool! how have they baffled[309] thee!

CLOWN. Why, *some are born great, some achieve greatness, and some have greatness thrown upon them.* I was one, sir, in this interlude,—one Sir Topas, sir; but that's all one:—*By the Lord,*

---

[307] *Geck* is from the Saxon *geac*, a cuckoo, and here means a *fool.*—Here, as twice before in this play, *notorious* is used, apparently, for *egregious.*

[308] *Importance* for *importunity.* So, in *King Lear*, iv. 4: "Therefore great France my mourning and *important* tears hath pitied."

[309] To treat with mockery or insult, to run a rig upon, and to make a butt of, are among the old senses of *baffle.*

fool, I am not mad;—But do you remember? *Madam, why laugh
you at such a barren rascal? An you smile not, he's gagged*: and
thus the whirligig of time brings in his revenges.

MALVOLIO. I'll be revenged on the whole pack of you. [*Exit.*]

OLIVIA. He hath been most notoriously abus'd.

DUKE. Pursue him, and entreat him to a peace:—
    He hath not told us of the captain yet;
    When that is known, and golden time convents,[310]
    A solemn combination shall be made
    Of our dear souls. Meantime, sweet sister,
    We will not part from hence.—Cesario, come:
    For so you shall be while you are a man;
    But, when in other habits you are seen,
    Orsino's mistress, and his fancy's queen.

[*Exeunt all but the* CLOWN.]

CLOWN.

SONG.

When that I was and[311] *a little tiny boy,*
    With hey, ho, the wind and the rain,
A foolish thing was but a toy,
    For the rain it raineth every day.

But when I came to man's estate,
    With hey, ho, the wind and the rain,
'Gainst knave and thief men shut their gate,[312]
    For the rain it raineth every day.

But when I came, alas! to wive,
    With hey, ho, the wind and the rain,
By swaggering could I never thrive,
    For the rain it raineth every day.

---

[310] *Convents* is *agrees* or *comes fit*; a Latinism.

[311] This redundant use of *and* is not uncommon in old ballads.

[312] "When I was a boy, my mischievous pranks were little regarded; but, when I
grew to manhood, men shut their doors against me as a *knave* and a *thief.*" *Gate* and *door*
were often used synonymously.

> *But when I came unto my bed,*
>   *With hey, ho, the wind and the rain,*
> *With toss-pots still had drunken head,*[313]
>   *For the rain it raineth every day.*

> *A great while ago the world begun,*
>   *With hey, ho, the wind and the rain,*
> *But that's all one, our play is done,*
>   *And we'll strive to please you every day.* [*Exit.*]

THE END

---

[313] "I had my head drunk with tossing off pots or drams of liquor." So a grog-shop is sometimes called a pot-house; and to *toss* is still used for to *drink*.